my **revision** notes

OCR A Level

RELIGIOUS STUDIES

DEVELOPMENTS IN CHRISTIAN THOUGHT

Chris Eyre

Julian Waterfield

HODDER
EDUCATION
AN HACHETTE UK COMPANY

Orders: please contact Bookpoint Ltd, 130 Park Drive, Milton Park, Abingdon, Oxon OX14 4SE. Telephone: (44) 01235 827720. Fax: (44) 01235 400401. Email education@bookpoint.co.uk Lines are open from 9 a.m. to 5 p.m., Monday to Saturday, with a 24-hour message answering service. You can also order through our website: www.hoddereducation.co.uk

ISBN: 978 1 5104 1806 6

© Julian Waterfield and Chris Eyre 2018

First published in 2018 by
Hodder Education,
An Hachette UK Company
Carmelite House
50 Victoria Embankment
London EC4Y 0DZ

www.hoddereducation.co.uk

Impression number   10 9 8 7 6 5 4 3 2

Year   2022   2021   2020   2019   2018

Cover photo © Delpixel/Shutterstock.com

Typeset by Integra Software Services, Pvt, Ltd, Pondicherry, India

Printed in Spain by Graphycems

A catalogue record for this title is available from the British Library.

Get the most from this book

Everyone has to decide his or her own revision strategy, but it is essential to review your work, learn it and test your understanding. These Revision Notes will help you to do that in a planned way, topic by topic. Use this book as the cornerstone of your revision and don't hesitate to write in it – personalise your notes and check your progress by ticking off each section as you revise.

Tick to track your progress

Use the revision planner on pages iv–vi to plan your revision, topic by topic. Tick each box when you have:

● revised and understood a topic
● tested yourself
● practised the 'Now test yourself' questions and checked your answers.

You can also keep track of your revision by ticking off each topic heading in the book. You may find it helpful to add your own notes as you work through each topic.

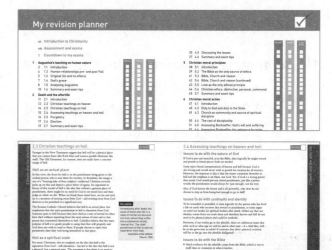

Features to help you succeed

Exam tips and checklists

Expert tips are given throughout the book to help you polish your exam technique in order to maximise your chances in the exam. The exam checklists provide a quick-check bullet list for each topic.

Typical mistakes

The author identifies the typical mistakes candidates make and explains how you can avoid them.

Now test yourself

These short, knowledge-based questions provide the first step in testing your learning. Answers are provided online.

Key terms

Clear, concise definitions of essential key words are provided where they first appear.

Key words from the specification are highlighted in bold throughout the book.

Key quotes

Quotations from prominent figures and key texts help your understanding of the content.

Revision activities

These activities will help you to understand each topic in an interactive way.

Making links

Useful links are provided to other topics within the specification.

Online

Go online to check your answers to the Now test yourself questions at **www.hoddereducation. co.uk/myrevisionnotes**.

My revision planner

vii **Introduction to Christianity**

viii **Assessment and exams**

1 **Countdown to my exams**

| | | REVISED | TESTED | EXAM READY |

1 Augustine's teaching on human nature
2 1.1 Introduction
4 1.2 Human relationships pre- and post-Fall
5 1.3 Original Sin and its effects
7 1.4 God's grace
8 1.5 Analysing Augustine
10 1.6 Summary and exam tips

2 Death and the afterlife
11 2.1 Introduction
12 2.2 Christian teachings on heaven
14 2.3 Christian teachings on hell
15 2.4 Assessing teachings on heaven and hell
16 2.5 Purgatory
17 2.6 Election
19 2.7 Summary and exam tips

3 Knowledge of God's existence
20 3.1 Introduction
21 3.2 Natural knowledge of God's existence
23 3.3 Revealed knowledge of God's existence
25 3.4 Has the Fall completely removed all natural human knowledge of God?
26 3.5 Is belief in God's existence sufficient to put one's trust in him?
27 3.6 Is natural knowledge of God the same as revealed knowledge of God?
28 3.7 Summary and exam tips

4 The person of Jesus Christ
29 4.1 Introduction
30 4.2 Jesus the Son of God
31 4.3 Jesus as a teacher of wisdom
33 4.4 Jesus as a liberator

REVISED TESTED EXAM READY

35 4.5 Discussing the issues

37 4.6 Summary and exam tips

5 Christian moral principles

38 5.1 Introduction

39 5.2 The Bible as the only source of ethics

41 5.3 Bible, Church and reason

42 5.4 Bible, Church and reason (continued)

43 5.5 Love as the only ethical principle

44 5.6 Christian ethics: distinctive, personal, communal

45 5.7 Summary and exam tips

6 Christian moral action

47 6.1 Introduction

48 6.2 Duty to God and duty to the State

49 6.3 Church as community and source of spiritual discipline

50 6.4 The cost of discipleship

51 6.5 Assessing Bonhoeffer: God's will and suffering

52 6.6 Assessing Bonhoeffer: his relevance for today

54 6.7 Summary and exam tips

7 Religious pluralism

55 7.1 Introduction

56 7.2 Exclusivism

57 7.3 Inclusivism

58 7.4 Pluralism

59 7.5 Discussing theology of religion

60 7.6 Inter-faith dialogue

62 7.7 The scriptural reasoning movement

64 7.8 Discussing inter-faith dialogue

65 7.9 Summary and exam tips

8 Gender

66 8.1 Introduction

67 8.2 Gender and gender roles

68 8.3 Christian teaching on the roles of men and women in the family and society

Yr12

		REVISED	TESTED	EXAM READY
69	8.4 Motherhood/parenthood	☐	☐	☐
70	8.5 Different types of family	☐	☐	☐
71	8.6 Reinterpretation of God by feminist theologians: Rosemary Radford Ruether	☐	☐	☐
73	8.7 Reinterpretation of God by feminist theologians: Mary Daly	☐	☐	☐
74	8.8 Comparing Ruether and Daly	☐	☐	☐
75	8.9 Assessing gender and theology	☐	☐	☐
76	8.10 Summary and exam tips	☐	☐	☐

9 The challenge of secularism

		REVISED	TESTED	EXAM READY
78	9.1 Introduction	☐	☐	☐
79	9.2 The view that society would be happier without Christianity	☐	☐	☐
80	9.3 The view that Christian belief should play no part in public life	☐	☐	☐
81	9.4 Is Christianity a major cause of personal and social problems?	☐	☐	☐
82	9.5 Are secularism and secularisation opportunities for Christianity?	☐	☐	☐
83	9.6 Assessing secularism	☐	☐	☐
84	9.7 Summary and exam tips	☐	☐	☐

10 Liberation theology and Marx

		REVISED	TESTED	EXAM READY
86	10.1 Introduction	☐	☐	☐
87	10.2 Marx's teachings	☐	☐	☐
88	10.3 Liberation theology	☐	☐	☐
90	10.4 Assessing liberation theology	☐	☐	☐
92	10.5 Summary and exam tips	☐	☐	☐

| 93 | **Glossary** | | | |

Introduction to Christianity

What is this book about?

Christianity, as we know it, is very different from the Christianity of the first century. And Christianity as one person knows it today could be very different to how another person in this country, let alone another country, knows it. This paper is about understanding the different approaches taken to Christianity and to try to get a sense of what sort of religion it needs to be as we move further into the twenty-first century.

The world is changing:
● people's priorities
● the ways we interact with each other
● who we interact with – and where they come from
● the pace and speed of life
● how easily we trust in things to do with faith
● the importance of science and reason.

But some things for Christians don't change:
● the role of God in the world
● the dignity of every human being
● the origins and consequences of sin
● what Jesus said and did
● what Jesus intended the Church to be like
● what happens when we die.

This paper challenges you to bring the two together. Theology is the study of religions; this paper focuses on Christianity, a religion full of different approaches, plenty of history and many colourful figures. At the heart of Christianity is the extremely colourful figure of Jesus Christ. What did the Christ-event actually do to the world?

What is theology?

If you were to choose a theology degree at university, you could find yourself exploring a range of religions or focusing on one religion, often Christianity. If it were a Christianity-based degree, you might do a number of papers on the Bible, or on key beliefs, or on Church history. You could look at sociology or psychology of religion, or worship or architecture; philosophy and ethics, archaeology, mythology and so on. This paper begins to touch on many of these aspects and different teachers will approach different topics in different ways. The examiner will be trained to give marks to what is right in your essays, even if you have been taught differently from someone else.

Enjoy it!

There will always be subtopics that you find harder than others, or that you just cannot get along with – but always make the most of your opportunity to study these topics – read around, search for key words on the internet and see what you find.

This paper is different to the other two papers you study. Philosophy and ethics are both part of the same branch of study; this is a different branch. The way you use your skills in the Christianity paper might be slightly different. Your essays will feel slightly different – the discussion might be broader than a philosophy essay; more historical than an ethics essay. Don't worry – just like the other two papers, if you are answering the question, using a range of points and arguments, you will be doing just fine.

If you are a Christian, you might find some of the conversations quite awkward or challenging – you might feel that your faith is under the spotlight. Enjoy the opportunity to develop your beliefs. If you are of another faith tradition, you might find it hard to empathise with where Christians are coming from. Enjoy finding links with your own religion and understanding big questions from a different perspective. If you don't follow a religion, you might find yourself looking from the outside inwards sometimes. Enjoy examining one of the biggest influences on the western world.

Assessment and exams

How the assessment objectives work depends on whether you are studying Religious Studies for AS- or A-level. If you are doing an AS course then there is no level 6 and the marks are split evenly between AO1 and AO2. If you are doing an A-level course, then 60 per cent of the marks are for AO2. The difference in weightings does not affect the advice in this book, nor what makes an essay a good essay: you do not have to do anything different at A-level to AS-level, it's just that how good you are at the different skills is given a different number of marks. Equally, don't feel you have to separate out AO1 and AO2 – write a series of great paragraphs and trust the marker to filter things out!

At AS-level, your exam is 1 hour and 15 minutes and you have to do two questions (from a choice of three). At A-level, your exam is 2 hours and you have to do three questions (from a choice of four). *If you are doing the AS-level, you only need Chapters 1–6 of this book; you will need all ten chapters for the full A-level.* Allowing time for settling down and choosing your questions, you basically have 35 minutes at AS-level and not much more at A-level for an essay. That doesn't seem much, but remember that the examiner will be aware of this.

Assessment objective 1: Knowledge and understanding

You will be able to see here that the marks are gained for being able to choose the right information to help you to answer the question. Better essays come from being more precise and knowing a useful range of material which you can explain concisely. The levels of response mark scheme for AO1 is included below.

Level (Mark)	Levels of response: Assessment objective 1 (AO1)
6 (14–16)	An **excellent** demonstration of knowledge and understanding in response to the question: ● fully comprehends the demands of, and focuses on, the question throughout ● excellent selection of relevant material which is skilfully used ● accurate and highly detailed knowledge which demonstrates deep understanding through a complex and nuanced approach to the material used ● thorough, accurate and precise use of technical terms and vocabulary in context ● extensive range of scholarly views, academic approaches and/or sources of wisdom and authority are used to demonstrate knowledge and understanding
5 (11–13) (AS: 13–15)	A **very good** demonstration of knowledge and understanding in response to the question: ● focuses on the precise question throughout ● very good selection of relevant material which is used appropriately ● accurate, and detailed knowledge which demonstrates very good understanding through either the breadth or depth of material used ● accurate and appropriate use of technical terms and subject vocabulary ● a very good range of scholarly views, academic approaches, and/or sources of wisdom and authority are used to demonstrate knowledge and understanding
4 (8–10) (AS: 10–12)	A **good** demonstration of knowledge and understanding in response to the question: ● addresses the question well ● good selection of relevant material, used appropriately on the whole ● mostly accurate knowledge which demonstrates good understanding of the material used, which should have reasonable amounts of depth or breadth ● mostly accurate and appropriate use of technical terms and subject vocabulary ● a good range of scholarly views, academic approaches and/or sources of wisdom and authority are used to demonstrate knowledge and understanding

→

Now test yourself answers at **www.hoddereducation.co.uk/myrevisionnotes**

Level (Mark)	Levels of response: Assessment objective 1 (AO1)
3 (5–7) (AS: 7–9)	A **satisfactory** demonstration of knowledge and understanding in response to the question: • generally addresses the question • mostly sound selection of mostly relevant material • some accurate knowledge which demonstrates sound understanding through the material used, which might however be lacking in depth or breadth • generally appropriate use of technical terms and subject vocabulary • a satisfactory range of scholarly views, academic approaches, and/or sources of wisdom and authority are used to demonstrate knowledge and understanding with only partial success
2 (3–4) (AS: 4–6)	A **basic** demonstration of knowledge and understanding in response to the question: • might address the general topic rather than the question directly • limited selection of partially relevant material • some accurate, but limited, knowledge which demonstrates partial understanding • some accurate, but limited, use of technical terms and appropriate subject vocabulary • a limited range of scholarly views, academic approaches and/or sources of wisdom and authority are used to demonstrate knowledge and understanding with little success
1 (1–2) (AS: 1–3)	A **weak** demonstration of knowledge and understanding in response to the question: • almost completely ignores the question • very little relevant material selected • knowledge very limited, demonstrating little understanding • very little use of technical terms or subject vocabulary • very little or no use of scholarly views, academic approaches and/or sources of wisdom and authority to demonstrate knowledge and understanding
0 (0)	No creditworthy response

Assessment objective 2: Analysis and evaluation

AO2 is about your ability to argue in response to the question. Examiners are making an assessment of your 'extended response' – how well are you arguing? Can you show that you have thought about a range of different approaches to the issue in the question? Are you critical about all the points you offer? Do you develop the arguments you give rather than stating them and moving on? The levels of response mark scheme for AO2 is included below.

Level (Mark)	Levels of response: Assessment objective 2 (AO2)
6 (21–24)	An **excellent** demonstration of analysis and evaluation in response to the question: • excellent, clear and successful argument • confident and insightful critical analysis and detailed evaluation of the issue • views skilfully and clearly stated, coherently developed and justified • answers the question set precisely throughout • thorough, accurate and precise use of technical terms and vocabulary in context • extensive range of scholarly views, academic approaches and sources of wisdom and authority used to support analysis and evaluation *Assessment of extended response: There is an excellent line of reasoning, well-developed and sustained, which is coherent, relevant and logically structured.*

→

Level (Mark)	Levels of response: Assessment objective 2 (AO2)
5 (17–20) (AS: 13–15)	A **very good** demonstration of analysis and evaluation in response to the question: • clear argument which is mostly successful • successful and clear analysis and evaluation • views very well stated, coherently developed and justified • answers the question set competently • accurate and appropriate use of technical terms and subject vocabulary • a very good range of scholarly views, academic approaches and sources of wisdom and authority used to support analysis and evaluation *Assessment of extended response: There is a well-developed and sustained line of reasoning which is coherent, relevant and logically structured.*
4 (13–16) (AS: 10–12)	A **good** demonstration of analysis and evaluation in response to the question: • argument is generally successful and clear • generally successful analysis and evaluation • views well stated, with some development and justification • answers the question set well • mostly accurate and appropriate use of technical terms and subject vocabulary • a good range of scholarly views, academic approaches and sources of wisdom and authority are used to support analysis and evaluation *Assessment of extended response: There is a well-developed line of reasoning which is clear, relevant and logically structured.*
3 (9–12) (AS: 7–9)	A **satisfactory** demonstration of analysis and/evaluation in response to the question: • some successful argument • partially successful analysis and evaluation • views asserted but often not fully justified • mostly answers the set question • generally appropriate use of technical terms and subject vocabulary • a satisfactory range of scholarly views, academic approaches and sources of wisdom and authority are used to support analysis and evaluation with only partial success *Assessment of extended response: There is a line of reasoning presented which is mostly relevant and which has some structure.*
2 (5–8) (AS: 4–6)	A **basic** demonstration of analysis and evaluation in response to the question: • some argument attempted, not always successful • little successful analysis and evaluation • views asserted but with little justification • only partially answers the question • some accurate, but limited, use of technical terms and appropriate subject vocabulary • a limited range of scholarly views, academic approaches and sources of wisdom and authority to support analysis and evaluation with little success *Assessment of extended response: There is a line of reasoning which has some relevance and which is presented with limited structure.*
1 (1–4) (AS: 1–3)	A **weak** demonstration of analysis and evaluation in response to the question: • very little argument attempted • very little successful analysis and evaluation • views asserted with very little justification • unsuccessful in answering the question • very little use of technical terms or subject vocabulary • very little or no use of scholarly views, academic approaches and sources of wisdom and authority to support analysis and evaluation *Assessment of extended response: The information is communicated in a basic/unstructured way.*
0 (0)	No creditworthy response

Countdown to my exams

6–8 weeks to go

- Start by looking at the specification available from **www.ocr.org.uk**. Make sure you know exactly what material you need to revise and the style of the examination. Use the revision planner on pages iv–vi to familiarise yourself with the topics.
- Organise your notes, making sure you have covered everything on the specification. The revision planner will help you group your notes into topics.
- Work out a realistic revision plan that will allow you time for relaxation. Set aside days and times for all the subjects that you need to study, and stick to your timetable.
- Set yourself sensible targets. Break your revision down into focused sessions of around 40 minutes, divided by breaks. These Revision Notes organise the basic facts into short, memorable sections to make revising easier.

REVISED ☐

4–6 weeks to go

- Read through the relevant sections of this book and refer to the exam tips, typical mistakes and key terms. Tick off the topics as you feel confident about them. Highlight those topics you find difficult and look at them again in detail.
- Test your understanding of each topic by working through the 'Now test yourself' questions in the book. Look up the answers online.
- Make a note of any problem areas as you revise, and ask your teacher to go over these in class.
- Look at past papers. They are one of the best ways to revise and practise your exam skills. Write or prepare planned answers to the questions in the exam checklists in the book.
- Try different revision methods. For example, you can make notes using mind maps, spider diagrams or flashcards.
- Track your progress using the revision planner and give yourself a reward when you have achieved your target.

REVISED ☐

One week to go

- Try to fit in at least one more timed practice of an entire past paper and seek feedback from your teacher, comparing your work closely with the mark scheme.
- Check the revision planner to make sure you haven't missed out any topics. Brush up on any areas of difficulty by talking them over with a friend or getting help from your teacher.
- Attend any revision classes put on by your teacher. Remember, he or she is an expert at preparing people for examinations.

REVISED ☐

The day before the examination

- Flick through these Revision Notes for useful reminders – for example, the exam tips, typical mistakes and key terms.
- Check the time and place of your examination.
- Make sure you have everything you need – extra pens and pencils, tissues, a watch, bottled water, sweets.
- Allow some time to relax and have an early night to ensure you are fresh and alert for the examination.

REVISED ☐

My exam

Religious Studies: Developments in Christian Thought

Date: ....

Time: ....

Location: ....

1 Augustine's teaching on human nature

1.1 Introduction

REVISED

Is there a distinctive human nature?

What does it mean to be a human being? What is it that's essential to being a human? Are we essentially good or bad? Thomas Hobbes (1588–1679) said that human life is 'solitary, poor, nasty, brutish and short'. For Hobbes, that sums up the natural state of a human being and all that saves us is society, which makes us civilised. Jean-Jacques Rousseau (1712–1778) said that 'man is born free and everywhere he is in chains'. His view was the opposite: it is society (civilisation) that has messed humans up – the natural state of a human is good.

Augustine (354–430) had a different view: humans were created in the image of God, but at the **Fall**, **human nature** was irretrievably damaged and we spend our lives battling against this, shown through our relationship with **sin**. We shall see how the idea of **concupiscence** affects Augustine's thinking through the chapter.

> ### Key words
>
> **Fall** The moment when Adam and Eve disobeyed God by eating the fruit of the forbidden tree; humans are 'fallen' because of this moment
>
> **Human nature** The essential sense of what all humans are like; shared characteristics
>
> **Sin** Turning away from the will of God
>
> **Concupiscence** The idea that our natural perfected state has been wounded so that we are not bad, but always inclining towards sin

When considering if there is a distinctive human nature, apart from the work on Augustine, you might like to consider some of the following points:

- Evolution seems to suggest that human nature is moving away from the primitive.
- If human nature is based on civilisation, it is clear that this changes with different civilisations – perhaps this is an argument against Hobbes.
- Marx said we are essentially creative beings – this creativity adapts to the situations we are placed in and so different people will have different natures.
- Sartre said that we make our own essence through the choices we make – there is no basic human nature.

The specification says

Topic	Content	Key knowledge

Augustine's teaching on human nature	● Human relationships pre- and post-Fall	● Augustine's interpretation of *Genesis* 3 (the Fall), including:
		  – the state of perfection before the Fall and Adam and Eve's relationship as friends
		  – lust and selfish desires after the Fall

	● Original Sin and its effects on the will and human societies	● Augustine's teaching that Original Sin is passed on through sexual intercourse and is the cause of:
		  – human selfishness and lack of free will
		  – lack of stability and corruption in all human societies

	● God's grace	● Augustine's teaching that only God's grace, his generous love, can overcome sin and the rebellious will to achieve the greatest good (*summum bonum*)

Learners should have the opportunity to discuss issues related to Augustine's ideas on human nature, including:
● whether or not Augustine's teaching on a historical Fall and Original Sin is wrong
● whether or not Augustine is right that sin means that humans can never be morally good
● whether or not Augustine's view of human nature is pessimistic or optimistic
● whether or not there is a distinctive human nature.

Revision activity

Write down what you personally think about there being a distinctive human nature. Justify your point and then give a reason why someone might disagree. Keep this balanced approach in mind as you explore the topic.

Now test yourself

TESTED ☐

1 What is the relationship between human nature and concupiscence?

1.2 Human relationships pre- and post-Fall

The state of perfection before the Fall

According to *Genesis*, when God created humans he made them as the pinnacle of his creation in his 'image and likeness'. They lived in the Garden of Eden – a perfect paradise where all they had to do was name the animals and live their lives. They could eat from any vegetation, except for the fruit of the tree of knowledge of good and evil.

The state that Adam and Eve lived in can only be described as perfect harmony.
- They had everything they needed.
- There were no threats to their lives.
- They were in harmony with God: he used to walk in the garden with them.
- They lived in complete obedience to God.

Augustine interpreted these few verses of *Genesis* to say that there was perfect harmony between the human body, **will** and reason.

Adam and Eve's relationship

Augustine analysed the relationship between Adam and Eve to find:
- They were married as friends.
- They were friends with God and the rest of creation.
- Their friendship included reproduction.
- They would have had the pleasure of sex, but as friendship is a greater good than lust, the sex would have been without lust. Adam could use his balanced body, will and reason to make his body want to have sex when he wanted.

The Fall

In *Genesis* 3, we read the story of the Fall. The serpent (Satan) tempts Eve to eat from the tree of knowledge of good and evil; she does so and Adam follows suit. They realise they are naked, they hide from God, he finds out and they are duly punished. Augustine interprets the events of the Fall in a number of ways:
- The shame of nakedness and the punishment to Eve of lust and subordination defines male–female relationships post-Fall.
- Harmony is lost (humans lose their friendship with God and are banished from the garden) and self-love and generous love separate within the will – they pull humans in opposing directions.
- Augustine is clear that it is the will, not the body, that has been corrupted.

Lust and selfish desires after the Fall

For Augustine, the effect of the Fall is wide-ranging. Friendship can still exist and still be important, but it is less straightforward because the will has become clouded. The will therefore moves people away from the good – this is what Paul describes when he says, 'I do not understand what I do. For what I want to do I do not do, but what I hate I do' (*Romans* 7:15). Augustine interpreted this passage in his own life to refer to his need to overcome his sexual desires but says this applies to all of us – lust begins to rule human relationships. This lack of control over our desires, especially our lust, is concupiscence.

> **Key word**
>
> **Human will** For Augustine, given to humans by God at creation and used to make choices. It is driven by self-love and generous love, which work together to help people choose to love God properly

> **Now test yourself**
>
> 2 Why did Augustine believe that Adam and Eve had to be married as friends before the Fall?
>
> 3 Where can the account of the Fall be found in the Bible?
>
> 4 What is Paul saying in *Romans* 7?
>
> TESTED

> **Typical mistake**
>
> Don't tell Biblical stories in detail: focus essays critically on the question.

1.3 Original Sin and its effects

Effects on the will

For Augustine, **Original Sin**, which came into the world at the Fall, characterises human nature. In his terms, the will continues in its disharmony and therefore rebels. This is illustrated sexually: man loses his ability to control his sexual desires – not just during sex but also in his desire to have sex. Those who do not have the urge for sex are showing a will rebelling in other ways. It is important to understand that other thinkers see Original Sin as describing human nature, but Augustine saw it as changing it; therefore, from the Fall onwards, no human being is truly good, however much they do good things.

Augustine believed that Original Sin is passed on to all generations through sexual intercourse because all humans are united through being descendants of Adam and Eve and all are conceived as a result of lust (except Jesus). This is shown in concupiscence. The Roman Catholic Church still holds this view.

> **Key word**
>
> **Original Sin** The state that humans were brought into by the Fall, which was the first sin

> **Key quote**
>
> How did the sin of Adam become the sin of *all his descendants*? The whole human race is *in* Adam 'as one body of one man'. By this 'unity of the human race' all men are implicated in *Adam's sin*, as all are implicated in *Christ's justice*. Still, the transmission of original sin is a *mystery* that we cannot fully understand. But we do know by Revelation that Adam had received original holiness and justice not for himself alone, but for *all human nature*. By yielding to the tempter, Adam and Eve committed a *personal* sin, but this sin *affected* the human nature that they would then *transmit in a fallen state*. It is a sin which will be transmitted by propagation to all mankind, that is, by the transmission of a human nature *deprived* of original holiness and justice. And that is why original sin is called 'sin' only in an analogical sense: it is *a sin 'contracted' and not 'committed' – a state and not an act.*
>
> *Catechism of the Catholic Church*, 404, emphasis added

> **Revision activity**
>
> Use the long quotation to pick out the key aspects of Augustine's thinking that are now held by the Roman Catholic Church. The sections in italics might help. Can you explain each idea?

Augustine said that Original Sin was a double death:
- killing the friendship between God and humans
- becoming mortal, following the Fall.

Now test yourself

5 What does it mean to say that Original Sin is 'contracted' and not 'committed'?

Effects on human societies

Before the Fall, humanity was characterised by friendship and the leadership humans required was gentle. However, after the Fall, humans needed proper authority to control them and their rebellious wills: this is shown in the different types of leader through the Old Testament. Slavery was an example of the effect of the Fall on society.

Augustine spoke of society's need for peace – not heavenly peace, which humans cannot achieve, but earthly peace, which is temporary and is based around earthly, material interests. Society must strive for this limited form of peace by aiming for virtues such as self-control, which would never have been needed without the Fall. Christians should, however, keep in mind that there is a greater peace available to all. The Church is available to help people on this journey.

Analysing Augustine on Original Sin

Strengths	Weaknesses
Sexual desires seem to play a disproportionate part in human life	Augustine's account relies on a literal interpretation of the Adam and Eve story and it could be unfair for people to be tainted by an act from so long ago
The Roman Catholic Church says that humans are divided and need the help of God to develop	There does not seem to be space for humans to develop spiritually or morally in Augustine's account
Augustine's view seems to correspond with our own experiences of life – we are torn in different directions, even when they are wrong	Evolution implies that we are headed towards perfection (mutating into better species over time), not away from it
Freud also said that the libido is central to the motivation of humans	Dawkins said that Augustine's negative approach has led to a lot of human suffering as well as an over-emphasis on sexuality

Can humans ever be morally good?

Although the emphasis is that Original Sin is not the same as a day-to-day sin, Augustine is clear that everyone is corrupted by the event. In this case, is it actually possible for humans ever to be good? And if not, is there any point in living virtuous lives?

> **Revision activity**
>
> As you go through the strengths and weaknesses, make a note of the questions that come to mind – these can be good examples of personal analysis if the opportunity to use them in an essay comes up.

Augustine does not think this. He says that people need to keep in mind things beyond earth – both the heavenly peace and also what God can give directly: **grace**. It still seems unfair, however, for humans to be living lives that will always fall short and this raises key questions about the nature of God.

> **Key word**
>
> **Grace** God's generous, undeserved and free act of love for the world through Jesus (and despite concupiscence)

> **Making links**
>
> We discuss the nature of God in more detail in the Philosophy of Religion book, Chapter 7.

We saw in the introduction the debate between Hobbes and Rousseau about human nature. Augustine would reject both views because they fail to understand the turning point for humanity – the Fall. However, when we look at a newborn baby, it is very difficult to imagine it tainted by Original Sin and Rousseau would have agreed – we start with clear records that society messes up.

It also seems unfair for humanity to be defined almost entirely by the idea of sex. Many modern theologians see sex as a healthy part of what it is to be human and would suggest that Augustine was too consumed by his own guilt and his early life where he found it difficult to control his sexual desires. Even these theologians, however, would say that sex needs to be controlled in some ways.

> **Making links**
>
> Sex is a key topic in the ethics section. See the Religion and Ethics book, Chapter 9.

> **Revision activity**
>
> Use a mind map to break down the information in this section. Try to rank order the strengths and weaknesses raised.

It is possible also to argue that there is no one distinct human nature and therefore it is possible for some, but not all, humans to be good. Psychological experiments have shown that, placed in identical situations, humans react differently. In this case, it could be argued that the question of whether humans can ever be morally good remains unclear.

Now test yourself

TESTED ☐

6 How can evolution be used as a criticism of Augustine?

1.4 God's grace

REVISED ☐

Our free will is naturally limited by the fact that, in Augustine's eyes, people are tainted by concupiscence and so cannot choose the right action every time, even by the use of reason. God's grace can make right choices, however. God's grace is freely given to undeserving humans and is seen especially in the sacrifice made by Jesus on the cross.

> **Making links**
>
> Plato is considered in Chapter 1 of the Philosophy of Religion book.
>
> Augustine's view on evil as being a lack (or privation) of the *summum bonum* is considered in the Philosophy of Religion book, Chapter 6.

Humans can accept the grace of God, but as they continue to sin, Augustine believed that God elects some people to go to heaven; this is a sign of God's benevolence, that he is still prepared to let some people go to heaven. This underlines the belief that humans do not deserve grace (because of the Fall and Original Sin), but grace is the only thing that can save people from hell.

Inspired by Plato, Augustine talks about God's goodness being a greatest good (*summum bonum*) that is available only for some – it is part of God's nature. Goodness in this world is always temporary, whereas the *summum bonum* is eternal happiness only found in the permanent presence of God. No person can buy a place in heaven, it can only be given by grace.

> **Key word**
>
> *Summum bonum* Highest or greatest good

Now test yourself

TESTED ☐

7 Explain the importance of the *summum bonum* for Augustine.

Is Augustine's view of human nature pessimistic or optimistic?

Clearly, Augustine seems to give a pessimistic view of what it means to be human:

- We are tainted from the moment we are born.
- There is little opportunity to develop away from our fallen states and no total escape from it.
- Where there is such opportunity, it is only to pursue earthly peace, rather than true heavenly peace.
- Concupiscence is an extremely strong force that we cannot escape.
- His teaching about election and **predestination** (discussed in more detail in Chapter 2, Death and the afterlife) suggests that hell is a certainty for some from the moment of birth.
- We are not truly free beings.

His pessimism seems to come out of his early experiences in life, so might reflect his state of mind more than God's.

> **Key word**
>
> **Predestination** The idea that God chooses and guides some people to salvation

On the other hand, Augustine could be argued to be very optimistic about humans. There is something to look forward to – heavenly peace is achievable:

- God's grace is totally given to undeserving humanity.
- Jesus died on the cross to save humans from sin: he redeemed humans – paid the price for their sinful natures.
- The Church exists to help Christians on their journey, starting with the important moment of baptism that keeps the wound of Original Sin closed.
- Faith exists as a way to point people in the direction of the *summum bonum*.

Modern Christians who have accepted much of what Augustine said would consider themselves optimists. The Roman Catholic Church speaks of the happy fault of Adam – Adam's sin meant that the inexpressibly greater blessings of Jesus could be given to the world. Many Christians emphasise that from the moment of the Fall, God was working his mysterious goodness in the world and the joy of Jesus' resurrection overcomes all pessimism.

> **Now test yourself**   TESTED ☐
>
> 8 Why does the idea of grace make Augustine more optimistic than might be thought?

1.5 Analysing Augustine   REVISED ☐

While Augustine was writing, the thinking of Pelagius was gaining in popularity and Augustine tried to counteract Pelagius's view that it is possible to live a moral life. Some key differences between the two are illustrated in the table opposite.

> **Exam tip**
>
> When discussing a view that seems outdated to many modern ears, it is important not to dismiss it as just old-fashioned without providing evidence for that judgement.

Now test yourself answers at **www.hoddereducation.co.uk/myrevisionnotes**

	Augustine	Pelagius
Human nature	Human nature is damaged by the Fall. It is sinful.	Humans can't have a flawed nature. If we did, then God would be commanding the impossible when he asks humans to be holy.
Sin	Humans are incapable of avoiding sin. The will is now such that it has a tendency away from goodness.	Humans do not have to sin. It is theoretically possible for people to be good. Sin can only be sin if it is freely chosen. It must be possible (if difficult) for humans to live the perfect life without God's intervention.
Guilt and Original Sin	Adam's sin affects all people. The Fall transmits guilt to the whole human race. Human beings are sinful at birth.	We are all created in the same state as Adam. We are only responsible for our own sin. We become sinners not at birth but when we choose to sin.
Death	Death is the consequence and punishment for sin.	Death is a biological necessity but not a punishment.
Grace	Humans cannot do any good deeds except by God's grace.	God's grace assists people in doing the right thing and showing what is right and wrong but humans carry out the actions. Pelagius saw grace as the natural human faculties, given by God.
Salvation	Salvation is the free and unmerited gift of God. The parable of the workers (*Matthew* 20:1–16) shows God rewards how he pleases – the reward is not because of actions.	For Pelagius, humans use their free will to choose God – their actions in choosing to bring the reward. For Augustine and his followers, this sounds like Pelagius is downplaying the role of grace.
Suffering	All suffering is deserved – even infant deaths – as all are in Original Sin.	Augustine makes God sound arbitrary (random) in punishing innocent babies.
God	Shows his benevolence through grace. Is not to blame for evil because evil is an absence of good, not a thing in itself.	It would be unjust of God to condemn humans for something they could not help. He would not give instructions that could not be kept.
Jesus	Is the expression of God's grace.	Good people existed in the Old Testament. They lived before Jesus brought salvation into the world.

Pelagius felt that Augustine's views were leading people towards immoral behaviour but ultimately his views were condemned at a Church Council in 418 where Augustine's view was upheld: Original Sin is inherited, babies need to be baptised and humans can only be good through God's grace. With modern understanding of the origins of humanity showing that the Adam and Eve story might not be literally true, there may be a place for Pelagius's views in the twenty-first century.

Revision activity

Pick the three essential differences between Augustine and Pelagius that you might select to put into an essay. Try to structure them into a paragraph, using your own words.

Now test yourself

TESTED ☐

9 What does Pelagius say about how humans are created?

1.6 Summary and exam tips

Exam checklist

- Explain Augustine's view about how things changed at the Fall.
- Explain Augustine's teaching on Original Sin.
- Analyse Augustine's teaching on the effect of Original Sin on the will and human society.
- Evaluate Augustine's view on grace and the *summum bonum*.
- Critically analyse Augustine's view of humanity.
- Assess the idea that there is a distinctive human nature.

Sample work

A decent paragraph will show analysis in several places through the paragraph and not save it until all the information has been written out.

First attempt	Improvement
Augustine said that after the Fall humans lost their friendship with God. They also introduced Original Sin into the world, which tainted all future humans. This Original Sin is passed on because every person is conceived as a result of lust.	Augustine said that after the Fall humans lost their friendship with God that was shown in their close relationship with him in the Garden of Eden; the shame of nakedness embarrassed Adam and Eve and broke the friendship. This certainly reflects modern relationships between people. At this point, Original Sin was brought into the world and is passed on to future humans through sex, which is a result of lust. Lust was one of the punishments given to Eve after the Fall but many scholars would suggest that Augustine has placed too much emphasis on sex and lust in his writings.

Going further: The Fall as symbolic

For many Christians, especially given modern understandings of the Big Bang and evolution, which contradict *Genesis*, the Fall *symbolises* the state of humanity. Most Christians find key truths within *Genesis*, such as that God is *responsible* for the universe and life, which he created with order; that humans have a special role on the planet and they used their free will to reject what they'd be given, thus alienating themselves from God.

Augustine's view of the Fall as a single moment when human nature became tainted would be wrong. Perhaps *Genesis* illustrates human nature, meaning basic human nature is flawed.

- Perhaps life is a process of development, as suggested by Hick.
- Perhaps human nature only seems flawed because we are trying to compare it with the *summum bonum*, and it is not essentially flawed.
- Perhaps human nature is flawed simply because we are physical beings and not God. In this case, it might be possible to retain some of Augustine's points.

We could also say that the Genesis account illustrates the first act of sin that all humans inevitably make at some point in their lives. If this is the case then Original Sin is not passed on, but sinfulness can be seen as something common to humans which would affect human societies (as Rousseau suggested). Each human individual therefore needs God's grace to overcome this essential aspect of human nature.

Exam tip

Try to remain analytical when you are discussing the Fall, so keep in mind alternative explanations for the *Genesis* account.

Now test yourself answers at **www.hoddereducation.co.uk/myrevisionnotes**

2 Death and the afterlife

2.1 Introduction

What happens after we die is a fundamental question in religious studies. The Christian understanding of what the afterlife is like and who will go to heaven has looked very different over the two thousand years of Christianity.

In Jesus' parable on Final Judgement, 'The Sheep and the Goats' (*Matthew* 25:31–46), he explored some fundamental questions about the afterlife. Jesus talks of his own coming in the future as King to judge the world, referring to himself as the son of man. The table below helps you to consider the parable – how much should it be taken literally and how much is it a story that is warning people to adjust how they live their lives?

Part of the parable	Points to consider
'All the nations will be gathered'	● All people seem to be being judged, not just Christians ● Judgement seems to happen at the end of time
The nations will be separated (like a shepherd separating sheep from goats)	● Some will go to heaven and some to hell: both places seem to be realities in the parable
'Take your inheritance, the Kingdom prepared for you since the creation of the world'	● Heaven is part of God's plan for all of creation
People who have helped the hungry, thirsty, strangers, etc., are invited to heaven	● People who go to heaven have earned it ● Salvation seems to be based on actions, not beliefs
'Truly I tell you, whatever you did for one of the least of these brothers and sisters of mine, you did for me'	● Jesus is found in the outcast and needy ● Anyone could have helped the needy, but not everyone did
'Then they will go away to eternal punishment, but the righteous to eternal life'	● The option between heaven and hell does not seem to include purgatory ● Either option is eternal ● Both options seem to be physical places

The parable certainly seems to suggest that judgement will take place at the end of time; some Christians emphasise by contrast that we will be judged individually after death; others combine both views.

> **Exam tip**
>
> The parable not only talks about the certainty of judgement and an afterlife but also suggests that it is our actions that will determine what will get us into heaven. You can therefore use this parable in a number of areas of the course, as long as you use it to answer the specific question set.

The specification says

Topic	Content	Key knowledge

Death and the afterlife	● Christian teaching on:
	  – heaven
	  – hell
	  – purgatory
		● Different interpretations of heaven, hell and purgatory, including:
		  – heaven, hell and purgatory are actual places where a person may go after death and experience physical and emotional happiness, punishment or purification
		  – heaven, hell and purgatory are not placed by spiritual states that a person experiences as part of their spiritual journey after death
		  – heaven, hell and purgatory are symbols of a person's spiritual and moral life on Earth and not places or states after death

	● Election	● Different Christian views of who will be saved, including:
		  – limited election (that only a few Christians will be saved)
		  – unlimited election (that all people are called to salvation but not all are saved)
		  – universalist belief (that all people will be saved)

		● The above to be studied with reference to the key ideas in Jesus' parable on Final Judgement, 'The Sheep and the Goats' (*Matthew* 25:31–46)
	Learners should have the opportunity to discuss issues related to Christian ideas on death and the afterlife, including: ● whether or not God's judgement takes place immediately after death or at the end of time ● whether or not hell and heaven are eternal ● whether or not heaven is the transformation and perfection of the whole of creation ● whether or not purgatory is a state through which everyone goes.	

Now test yourself

TESTED ☐

1 Who does Jesus say will be judged at the end of time?

2.2 Christian teachings on heaven

REVISED ☐

The New Testament speaks confidently about heaven as a place of eternal reward for people. Our bodies, according to Paul, will be transformed at death into spiritual bodies and raised to a spiritual home. Jesus' own resurrection gives a glimpse into what this will be like. There is no reincarnation in Christianity – who we are now will be who we are in heaven, transformed by an act of God.

Traditional views

Thomas Aquinas spoke of heaven as a **beatific vision**. This is the moment when we come face-to-face with God and live in happiness and harmony with God for ever. Because we have intelligence and eternal souls, Aquinas thought that we can use our reason to reach the reward of this beatific vision. This view tends to be that held by Catholics.

Key word

Beatific vision The state of eternal happiness when we are face-to-face with God

Christians do not believe that heaven can ever be fully described and so we can only use our limited language to explore the idea. The Bible helps with this:

- a place where those who have worked for righteousness are
- a place where people like Abraham are, as well as the angels
- a place where there is no more hunger or pain
- a place where every tear is wiped away: there is no sadness.

Following this Biblical tradition, many Protestant Churches see heaven as everlasting, not eternal. Heaven is a place where people live for the rest of time in the presence of God, alongside their family and friends. They spend their time joined together in the worship of God. Catholics would not say that we are not 'with' our family and friends in heaven, but that the way we relate to other people will change.

Whichever view is followed, heaven is depicted as a permanent and very real place where a person experiences physical and emotional happiness. The evidence for it being like this comes mainly from the Bible – after all, where did Jesus go to?

Other views

Some might suggest that heaven is a natural continuation of our spiritual journey after death. If the body is not needed in the afterlife, and our souls capture who we are as people, then heaven does not need to be a 'place' as we understand the word and the word 'state' might be used – heaven is a different form of existence, rather than a place where we might go.

Heaven, therefore, becomes understood as the moment our souls leave our bodies behind to be with God in a non-physical sense. Some argue that this is more of the sort of heaven that Jesus described and that the idea of a physical place was added by Paul later.

New Testament scholar N.T. Wright suggests that when we understand the context of the Gospels, we understand that what was expected was a transformation of this present world into God's kingdom. This means that heaven is not to be found in another world, but in a future state of this world. The book of *Revelation* explores the transformation of this world in detail. In this case, it could be argued that at the end of time, Christ will come again (the **Parousia**) and all of creation will be transformed.

An alternative approach is that heaven is a symbol of a person's spiritual and moral life on earth. The idea here is that the person who has been worthy on earth of heaven has had moments of blissful happiness, both personally and in their interactions with other people. Heaven then becomes a representation of the sum of all positive moments in someone's life. Of course, in this model, heaven does not need to be a real place; perhaps it is captured in the memories of those we leave behind.

> **Key quote**
>
> This perfect life with the Most Holy Trinity – this communion of life and love with the Trinity, with the Virgin Mary, the angels and all the blessed – is called 'heaven'. Heaven is the ultimate end and fulfilment of the deepest human longings, the state of supreme, definitive happiness.
>
> *Catechism of the Catholic Church*, 1024

> **Making links**
>
> See Chapter 7 in the Philosophy of Religion book on the difference between eternal and everlasting and its implications.

> **Making links**
>
> In Chapter 2 of the Philosophy of Religion book, we consider the relationship between body and soul.

> **Key word**
>
> **Parousia** Used of the second coming of Christ, when Jesus will return to judge the world

Now test yourself

TESTED

2 What did Aquinas describe heaven as?
3 Which book of the New Testament describes the transformation of this world to a heavenly world?

2.3 Christian teachings on hell

Passages in the New Testament suggest that hell will be a physical place that you cannot leave (the Rich Man and Lazarus parable illustrates this well). The Old Testament, by contrast, does not really have a concrete image of hell.

Hell as an actual place

In this view, the focus for hell is on the punishment being given to the wicked person who is sent there for eternity. In *Revelation*, the image is one of a 'burning lake of fiery sulphur'; traditional Christian artwork picks up on this and depicts a place below of agony. An argument in favour of this model of hell is the idea that without a genuine place of punishment, there might be no need for God to set moral laws and then judge us when we die. When we break those moral laws, we sin and each sin is a moment of turning away from God – and turning away from God deserves to be punished in a significant way.

The Roman Catholic Church believes that hell is an actual place, but emphasises that the main punishment in hell is alienation from God. Someone goes to hell because they have died in a state of mortal sin (they have died without repenting from the most serious of sins) and so that person has committed themselves to hell. Catholics believe that the main purpose of hell is to guide people to using their free will properly and God does not wish to send us there. If people choose to reject him persistently then they will bring themselves to that place.

Hell as a spiritual state

For many Christians, this re-emphasis on the idea that hell is the separation from God – self-alienation – has led to the idea that hell is not a physical, but a spiritual state. The argument is that there is no need to be punished by fire because alienation from God would be punishment enough. Biblical and medieval images are simply products of their time – after all, we know that hell is not a place in the depths of the earth. Paul Tillich is an example of a theologian who has understood hell as a metaphor of psychological alienation.

Hell in symbolic terms

Much like the views on heaven above, it could be simply that hell is a symbolic representation of the negative elements of someone's life. Other people think that because a loving God would not subject people to eternal punishment, hell might be a symbolic representation that if we are judged unworthy to go to heaven, we will be annihilated and our existence will not continue after bodily death. Some think of this as a second death because of the passage in *Revelation* 21:8 where being cast into the pit of fire is specifically called 'the second death'.

> **Key quote**
>
> Immediately after death the souls of those who die in a state of mortal sin descend into hell, where they suffer the punishments of hell, 'eternal fire'. The chief punishment of hell is eternal separation from God.
>
> *Catechism of the Catholic Church*, 1035

> **Revision activity**
>
> Make a mind map on heaven and hell, focusing on the afterlife being (1) real, (2) spiritual and (3) symbolic.

Now test yourself

4 What does the Roman Catholic Church say about God sending people to hell?
5 What word could be used to describe 'the second death'?

2.4 Assessing teachings on heaven and hell

Issues to do with the nature of God

If God is just and merciful, as in the Bible, then logically he might reward and punish in literal places: both are needed.

Some reject literal interpretations of heaven and hell because God is also loving and would never wish to punish his creation for all eternity. However, the response to this is that the sinner condemns *themselves* to hell and the emphasis is on them, not God. Yet, if God is a loving parent then surely God would prevent *eternal* punishment, just like a parent would; the punishment would always be 'just enough', not for ever.

Also, if God knows the future and is all-powerful, why does he not choose to stop us from being bad enough to go to hell?

Issues to do with continuity and identity

To be rewarded or punished, it must logically be the person who has lived a life on earth who receives that reward or punishment, so some argue we need our bodies (or spiritual bodies) after death. Others say that our identity comes from our souls alone and therefore heaven and hell do not need to be physical places and could be symbolic.

However, if our bodies go to the afterlife, there are additional issues that arise, such as what age we will be and in what state – if a child dies, will he or she grow into an adult? If someone dies after a physical accident, will he or she go into the afterlife disfigured?

Issues to do with the Bible

- Much evidence for the afterlife comes from the Bible, which is not in itself clear or consistent in what it teaches.
- Not all Christians believe that the Bible needs to be taken literally, so any symbolic understanding of the Bible might lead to a symbolic understanding of issues to do with the afterlife.
- However, the Bible does suggest that there is *something* after death, and so some would reject any view that challenges this.

Issues to do with believability

Some suggest that it does not make sense that there is one punishment (and one reward) for the full range of possible lives that people lead. It is not believable to suggest that one sin leads to hell and equally not easy to determine when someone has sinned enough to be punished.

Some also observe that any form of heaven that includes the passage of time would become boring because there would be nothing to do! Aquinas' response would be that at the beatific vision all our attitudes will change, including our relationship with time.

Another issue with believability is that any idea of heaven and hell as physical places begs the question 'where are they?'.

Christians who have put their trust in a God who made the universe and rose again from the dead in Jesus would say that believing in heaven is not as hard as other basic Christian beliefs. Some might also observe that the idea of heaven and hell is found in other faith traditions and so there is likely to be an essential truth that is behind the belief.

> **Revision activity**
>
> Which of these arguments do you find most persuasive? Least persuasive? Try to summarise them in your own words and say why you feel that way about the arguments.

> **Now test yourself**
>
> 6 Why might the nature of God be an argument against hell?
> 7 Why is identity important when considering the afterlife?
>
> TESTED

2.5 Purgatory

Purgatory is a state of cleansing that takes place before someone enters heaven. If someone is judged to have been 'good' at death, but not perfect, then they undergo purgatory before entering heaven. It is a Catholic view that acknowledges that most people are not bad enough for hell, but no one on earth is worthy to meet God face-to-face in their current state. Catholics believe the efforts you make on earth (such as going to Confession) to make up for your sins can have a positive impact on the next life.

Protestant Christians often say that there is no direct Biblical evidence for this. Catholics point to:

- 2 *Maccabees* 12, which says that we should pray for the dead, implying we can make a difference to someone who has died (the problem is that this book is in the Catholic version of the Old Testament, not the Protestant version).
- *Matthew* 12, which talks about sins against the Holy Spirit not being forgiven in this age or the age to come (suggesting that some sins can be forgiven in the age to come).
- Biblical references to cleansing by fire (the cleansing in purgatory traditionally was said to take place by fire), for example, 1 *Corinthians* 3.

The idea of some sort of purgatory was certainly present in the Early Church. Origen (184–254) talked about some sort of opportunity for the soul to perfect itself. The Church's view comes more from the teaching of Gregory of Nyssa (c.335–c.395), who saw it as tying in with the idea of a God who wanted as many people to come to heaven as possible.

John Hick is an example of a liberal theologian who saw value in the idea of purgatory. Hick felt that hell could not be part of a loving God's plan and so thought that there must be an opportunity after death for all to be purified before heaven.

It could be that purgatory should be understood less as a place of pain and more as a spiritual state where a person comes to a greater understanding of their sinfulness, perhaps between individual judgement and final judgement. Alternatively, purgatory could be symbolic of the final moment of repentance when we are presented with the eternal, perfect nature of God.

Some arguments against purgatory might be:

- The sacrifice of Jesus on the cross was enough to enable people to enter heaven, or, at least, for those who have accepted Jesus into their lives.
- Belief in purgatory led to corruption in the Middle Ages where it was felt you could buy your way out of some of the cleansing fire (the sale of indulgences was one of the reasons for the Reformation).
- It is not clear how the cleansing might work if heaven and hell are spiritual places.
- If heaven and hell are eternal, then how can purgatory be a place where you go for an amount of time?

Key word

Purgatory The (mainly) Catholic belief in a state of cleansing that takes place before someone enters heaven

Key quote

All who die in God's grace and friendship, but still imperfectly purified, are indeed assured of their eternal salvation; but after death they undergo purification, so as to achieve the holiness necessary to enter the joy of heaven.

Catechism of the Catholic Church, 1030

Typical mistake

Purgatory is often misunderstood as being a state prior to judgement.

Now test yourself

TESTED

8 State three possible pieces of Biblical evidence for purgatory.

The discussion about **election** is about who will be saved. Primarily, election means that God knows where we will go when we die and has known this since before our birth. It makes logical sense, given that God is omniscient. Some forms of the doctrine of election have God making the choice himself.

Limited election

This view originally comes from Augustine, who said that Original Sin has created such a hold on humanity that God's grace is required for salvation – and God's grace must be given by God so God is in control of the decision. Augustine might have referred to *Matthew* 22:14, which says that 'many are invited but few are chosen'.

This was taken up by John Calvin, the influential sixteenth-century Protestant reformer, who, in affirming God's ultimate control over all things, could not envisage God being anything except in control of both the free choices we make and therefore the eternal life we will enter into, good or bad (**double predestination**).

Calvin thought:
- We should not presume to work out the will of God; God knows our limitations.
- Christians must behave as if all people are called because we do not know whom God has chosen; this includes the people to whom Christians choose to preach.
- Morality is still central because it reaffirms our position in the next life and the elect may reflect on the fact that they are still sinners, chosen because of God's grace.

The Roman Catholic Church stresses the choice of humans and says that bad people send themselves to hell. God knows that some people will fulfil their calling to be the best they can be and so these are the people he chooses to go to heaven. This is still a form of predestination and technically **limited election**, often known as **single predestination**.

Unlimited election

Unlimited election suggests first and foremost that heaven is available to all, but still emphasises the possibility of not everyone being saved. The idea comes from Karl Barth, who said:
- Jesus by being God-made-human was both the one who elects and also the one who is elected. This means that all humans may be saved because Jesus has taken on our human form.
- The choice that God made is not the choice of who to save, but the choice of God coming to earth as Jesus.
- All people are elected through Jesus taking on the punishment of death: 'There is no condemnation – literally none – for those that are in Christ Jesus' (Barth, *Church Dogmatics*).

Key word

Election Being chosen by God for heaven or hell

Key quote

For those God foreknew he also predestined to be conformed to the image of his Son.

Romans 8:29

Key words

Double predestination The view (held by Calvinists) that God chooses those who will go to heaven and also those who will go to hell

Limited election The view that only some people are chosen to be saved

Single predestination The view (held by Catholics) that God chooses those who will go to heaven

Unlimited election The view that everyone is called to be saved but only a few will be

Universalism

Barth's views are often taken to imply that he was a universalist – that is, he believed that everyone would go to heaven and, indeed, he refused to deny this. However, **universalism** teaches that it is necessary that everyone goes to heaven; Barth insisted that it was not necessary, but that the free choice of God ensures that heaven is open to all.

John Hick's view was that everyone necessarily must go to heaven because that is the only way that a loving God could logically exist in the world. In the afterlife, there will be the opportunity to finish the soul-making process and everyone will get there eventually. However, Hick is often criticised for giving the impression that it does not matter what choices we make; morality would perhaps become unnecessary. Hick also does not seem to give sufficient emphasis to Jesus' sacrifice on the cross.

When does judgement take place?

Whether or not we are chosen by God for heaven or we make our afterlife for ourselves, Christianity is clear that we will go through judgement. The earliest Christians saw judgement as a future event, a Day of Judgement, when all will enter heaven or hell. This is the image we see in the parable of the Sheep and the Goats. While we wait for this moment, people exist in a neutral, but positive, state, perhaps a bit like sleep.

However, the Bible seems to suggest that people might go straight to heaven or hell. When talking to the thief on the cross, Jesus seems to say that today he would be with Jesus in paradise. This could, of course, reflect the fact that after death, time will need to be understood differently.

Modern Christians tend to talk about our own **particular judgement**, which will then lead to a **final judgement** for all of creation.

Different Christian views of who will be saved: analysis

Universalism seems to remove free will from humans and yet limited election does not seem to tie in with belief in a God of love. It could be argued that God chooses where we go for eternity because of his foreknowledge of our actions, putting the emphasis on humans. Calvin would have said that it is presumptuous to say to God, 'I deserve salvation' and so for him the most important thing to protect was God's control over the situation; he would have rejected the idea that election suggests God does not love us and would instead, with Augustine, have emphasised the idea of God's grace.

Calvin developed the idea of a neutral state to say that those whom God has chosen will exist in a positive state and those rejected by God would be in pain. If this view is taken, then all of creation can be said to come around in a circle, back to the perfect state at the start of *Genesis*. It is difficult in this situation to explain how limited election might have been part of a plan to redeem humanity and to restore all of creation.

Key words

Universalism The view that everyone will be saved

Particular judgement Individual judgement at the moment of death

Final judgement The judgement of all nations at the end of time

Revision activity

Make a table with three columns to compare limited election, unlimited election and universalism.

Exam tip

Discussion about election has not been a part of the Catholic tradition and was mainly introduced into Christianity through Calvin's emphasis on the teachings of Augustine. The Protestant preference for revelation, rather than reason, also places much of the emphasis on God, rather than on humans, so it is possible to understand why Protestants concern themselves more with this debate and Catholics focus on the choices humans make.

Now test yourself

9 Which scholars would be associated with limited election, unlimited election and universalism?

TESTED ☐

Exam checklist

- Explain different beliefs about heaven.
- Explain different beliefs about hell.
- Explain Christian views about purgatory.
- Explain limited election, unlimited election and universalism.
- Critically evaluate whether heaven, hell and purgatory are real places.
- Assess which view about election is correct.
- Explore Christian ideas about judgement.

Sample work

Start by writing arguments for and against the statement or issue in the question. Then, next to the arguments, write down which key information you might include in each part. Finally, select which sections you will write about. In the example below, we imagine a question asking you to evaluate Christian beliefs about election and focus on just a small part of the plan. The whole plan should take just two or three minutes but can save you from running out of time!

> **Exam tip**
>
> Planning essays seems like a difficult thing to justify in 35 minutes, but the reality is that you should have more information and more arguments than you can possibly hope to write down in the time available. It's therefore important to use a plan to decide which of the many things you could write about are going to go in your essay.

First attempt	Improvement	
	For	**Against**
● Limited election ● Unlimited election ● Universalism	God is in control (Calvin)	God is a God of love (Hick)
	Bible says many are called but few are chosen (Augustine)	God sent Jesus (Barth)

Going further: The Sheep and the Goats

Sometimes, a deeper reading of a passage can help understand the context in which it was told. Here are some further thoughts about the parable of Final Judgement in *Matthew* 25:

- In certain contexts, it is hard to tell the difference between a sheep and a goat: reminding us that we cannot always know if our neighbour is good or bad, but Jesus knows us inside and out!
- Shepherds used the curve of their crook to protect their sheep. Perhaps the goats will be very firmly pulled away from the sheep, emphasising that their condemnation to hell is final. We also remember that Jesus, as a shepherd, is protecting us in some way.
- The context of the parable in *Matthew* chapters 24–25 is one of not leaving it too long to be ready for Jesus to come back, of taking every opportunity offered to you and of not knowing the time when God will come back. The parable reminds us that once we get to judgement there is no going back on our previous actions: now is the time to help others.
- Matthew's Gospel reminds us throughout of the importance of actions and Jesus warns against being like the Jewish authorities of the time who focused on talking but not doing.
- The following chapters show Jesus becoming one of the oppressed (the people that the 'sheep' helped) to die for the sins of the world as an innocent victim, portraying Jesus as having real authority to be the King who judges in this parable.

3 Knowledge of God's existence

3.1 Introduction

If I say I know something or someone or if I claim to know that 2 + 2 = 4, I am using the word 'know' in very different ways. I could be saying that my knowledge is logical, or that I am aware of some facts about something or alternatively that I have some sort of relationship with someone. It is important for theology to make sure that we are sure of what we mean when we say that we 'know' God. One of the major parts of this topic is to work out how we get that knowledge and how valid the different ways are of getting that knowledge. The two ways of understanding how we know God are **natural theology** and **revealed theology**.

The Roman Catholic Church sees both natural and revealed theology as important ways to know God. There are a range of views in Protestant Christianity but a key thinker, examined below, is John Calvin, whose views on natural theology in particular have been interpreted in different ways.

It is important to understand that these distinctions are not the only ways to explore the question of how humans can know God. Other Christian traditions emphasise the unknowability of God or the importance of contemplation in coming to meet with God spiritually. What is common to all, however, is that whatever *can* be known about God needs more than just reason or logic. God is very different to other things we might try to know.

> ### Key words
>
> **Natural theology** Use of reason and observation of the world to come to a knowledge of God
>
> **Revealed theology** The idea that God reveals what we need to know about him to us in different ways – for example, through the Bible or the person of Jesus

> ### Now test yourself
>
> 1 What are the definitions of natural theology and revealed theology?
>

The specification says

Topic	Content	Key knowledge
Knowledge of God's existence	● Natural knowledge of God's existence: – as an innate human sense of the divine	● As all humans are made in God's image they have an inbuilt capacity and desire to know God, including: – human openness to beauty and goodness as aspects of God – human intellectual ability to reflect on and recognise God's existence
	– as seen in the order of creation	● What can be known of God can be seen in the apparent design and purpose of nature
	● Revealed knowledge of God's existence: – through faith and God's grace	● As humans are sinful and have finite minds, natural knowledge is not sufficient to gain full knowledge of God; knowledge of God is possible through: – faith – grace as God's gift of knowledge of himself through the Holy Spirit
	– revealed knowledge of God in Jesus Christ	● Full and perfect knowledge of God is revealed in the person of Jesus Christ and through: – the life of the Church – the Bible
	Learners should have the opportunity to discuss issues related to Christian ideas on knowledge of God, including: ● whether or not God can be known through reason alone ● whether or not faith is sufficient reason for belief in God's existence ● whether or not the Fall has completely removed all natural human knowledge of God ● whether or not natural knowledge of God is the same as revealed knowledge of God ● whether or not belief in God's existence is sufficient to put one's trust in him.	

Now test yourself answers at **www.hoddereducation.co.uk/myrevisionnotes**

3.2 Natural knowledge of God's existence

In natural theology, the thinker tries to use reason and experience to understand God's nature and God's existence. The idea is that there is a point of contact between God and humans that can be discovered when analysing things around us. In *Romans* 1:18–21, Paul, when speaking about God's anger towards people's failings, says that they could have known God by understanding that creation tells us about God's invisible nature – they simply needed to think properly. This makes the point that it is possible to use the tools we have around us to come to conclusions about God.

Innate human sense of the divine

Many Christians speak of there being some sort of spark of God or the divine in each person. The Roman Catholic Church says that 'the desire for God is written in the human heart' (*Catechism of the Catholic Church*, 27), suggesting that imprinted in each person is a basic sense of God that gives them the capacity and desire to know God.

In the sixteenth century, the Protestant reformer John Calvin said a similar thing, that all people have an **innate *sensus divinitas*** (divine sense) that makes it possible for anyone to know God. He also spoke of the *semen religionis* (the seed of religion) that is found inside all people. Calvin thought that people are not fully aware of the *sensus divinitas* because they are confused by sin – it is sin, through human free choice, that makes people unable sometimes to recognise God.

Three key examples of how humans experience the *sensus divinitas* are:

1 The *conscience* – the feeling of guilt that we have inside us when we do something wrong is a voice inside us that provides innate evidence that God exists. This view of the conscience suggests that humans are open to understanding goodness as an aspect of God – goodness comes from God and we feel good or bad when we do good or bad things. Calvin said that the conscience is a capacity given by God and is part of the human response to God.

2 Humans are also aware of beauty and the Roman Catholic Church states that this appreciation of *aesthetics* helps people to understand God's existence. When we see a beautiful sight or hear a beautiful sound, we can use our reason to interpret this experience to understand that God is working in the world. Our ability to do this is a capacity that God has given us and from this realisation we can use our reason to learn about God and God's nature.

3 What sets humans apart from the rest of the world is our *intellectual* ability – our powers of reason. This reason can help us to reflect on what we see around us, such as the nature of objects, natural laws, as well as the fine-tuned design of the world to recognise God's existence. Thomas Aquinas is one of the most famous thinkers to use reason to justify the existence of God in his Five Ways, which many claim prove the existence of the Christian God. Even if they do not, theologians often argue that put together the Five Ways provide significant evidence that there is a God.

> **Key words**
>
> **Innate** Natural. An innate human sense of the divine is something we are born with, not one we acquire
>
> *Sensus divinitas* A sense of God, used by Calvin to talk about an innate sense in each of us

> **Key quote**
>
> There is within the human mind, and indeed by natural instinct, an awareness of divinity. This we take to be beyond controversy … God himself has implanted in all men a certain understanding of his divine majesty.
>
> John Calvin, *Institutes of the Christian Religion*, 1.3.1

> **Exam tip**
>
> Make sure you are able to talk about the range of thought within Christianity.

Natural knowledge of God's existence through the order of creation

Given the view that we have a basic understanding that beauty comes from God, reflecting on the beauty of creation – according to natural theologians – is a way of us experiencing something that leads us to God. Design arguments for the existence of God challenge us to use our reason to see if we can deduce that God exists from the beauty and intricacies of the world around us. Calvin sees the idea of the beauty of the earth as being like a mirror of God, reflecting his nature through the world – this is a bit like Paul's argument in *Romans* 1.

Design or *teleological arguments* also reflect on the idea of purpose in creation. The orderliness of the universe seems to show a higher purpose behind it and even modern views about evolution can be helped by suggesting that there is a force controlling the progress of evolution. Natural theology, therefore, does not need to be limited to pre-twentieth century understandings of the world. Calvin spoke of the 'principle of accommodation', which is the idea that God, despite being unknowable, has communicated with humans in ways that they will understand and in ways that they can work out.

Typical mistake

Don't make a theology essay into a philosophy essay and veer off into talking too much about the design argument. Always focus on the question!

Now test yourself

TESTED

2 List different points of contact between God and the world, according to natural theology.
3 What does the Roman Catholic Church say about natural theology?

Strengths

- Natural theology works in a way that we are used to. It is normal for humans to use their brains to reason.
- Furthermore, there is a long tradition, both within Christianity and outside it, that shows people using reason to show God exists.
- It is reasonable to suggest that the sheer number of people who have had some sort of faith suggests that there is a point of contact between God and humans.
- It is reasonable to believe that a God who lovingly created humans would have made some way for those humans to have contact with him.
- Appreciation of awe and wonder takes us beyond the physical and the feelings we experience seem to be on a level different to material things – this might point to a God that can be known from earthly things.

Weaknesses

- Is the gap just too great between humans and God to accept the *sensus divinitas*?
- Is natural theology of any use if we cannot gain personal knowledge of God: knowing God should be able to lead to a relationship with him?
- Many people use their reason to come up with different conclusions, including that God does not exist, so perhaps reason is not helpful and is too subjective.
- Order and purpose in nature can perhaps be explained by other factors, such as natural selection in the theory of evolution.
- Just because beauty makes us feel awe, it does not mean that God has made this feeling.

Revision activity

Rewrite these strengths and weaknesses in the order of most convincing down to least convincing.

3.3 Revealed knowledge of God's existence

Revealed theology looks at things the other way around to natural theology. Natural theology starts with human responses to what they see around them; revealed theology looks at what God has deliberately shown (revealed) to people. For Christians, the essentials of their faith have been given by God through **revelation**.

Revelation can be understood both in direct terms (when God reveals himself directly to a person or group of people) and in indirect terms (when God reveals himself via another source – a person, or perhaps the Bible).

> **Key word**
>
> **Revelation** Literally uncovering something that was previously hidden

Revelation through faith and God's grace

Christians do not believe that natural theology alone is enough to gain full knowledge of God because humans are sinful (because of the Fall, as well as their natures) and because human intellect is finite or limited. Roman Catholics see faith as being something that works alongside reason – it is about 'buying in' to something that you have reasoned to be true. True faith is something that comes through a process of formation where prayer and reflection allow a person to let go of reason alone. Aquinas reflected on the idea of faith at some length and he saw it as a conscious choice to accept something that is not certain – and so it is different from science. For Calvin, Christian faith comes properly through an acceptance of Jesus as the Redeemer of the world, which is done not on a rational level but at a spiritual level. Once people understand that Jesus is a special revelation of God's purpose for the world then, for Calvin, faith in Jesus leads towards true knowledge of God.

Grace is the word used to describe God's unconditional, constant and immense giving of goodness to the world; it is often referred to as 'undeserved favour'. It is not something humans can ask for. Christians believe that it is because of God's grace that they are given faith and it is because of God's grace that faith becomes a real, personal relationship with God.

Calvin said that the Holy Spirit helps humans in their lives by giving faith – the Holy Spirit acts in the world to give gifts, such as wisdom and understanding, and right judgement to open people up to faith and God's grace.

> **Key quote**
>
> The grace of God has no charms for men till the Holy Spirit gives them a taste for it.
>
> John Calvin, *Institutes of the Christian Religion*, 3.24.14

Revealed knowledge of God in Jesus Christ

Christianity hinges on the nature and actions of Jesus.
- For Catholics:
  - God's revelation was completed through the Christ-event and the sending of the Holy Spirit, but the way it is relevant today needs to be understood in each new circumstance.
  - This is the work of the Church: to explore God's revelation in the present day, to make it accessible to people and to enable them to access God's grace in their daily lives.
  - God is revealed through both the Bible and Church tradition.
  - The Church was a gift given by Jesus to the world to continue the work that Jesus began and to spread the good news about Jesus to the world.
  - The actions of the Church reveal aspects of God – for example, in the practice of certain rituals, such as the sacraments. For example, the Eucharist in Catholic belief makes present the sacrifice of Jesus to the worshipper who takes part in the service.

- For most Protestants:
  - The Bible holds more authority than the Church.
  - The Church's role is generally seen to point believers towards the revelation found in the Bible.
  - Calvin emphasised the work of Jesus on the cross – Jesus bridged the gap between humans and God, created at the Fall, and redeemed the world. It is this idea of Jesus as Mediator and Redeemer that Calvin returns to again and again.

The Bible tells the story of salvation history – the plan of action put in place by God to redeem humanity through Jesus.

- God works through history to bring his people to a place where they can fully understand the person of Jesus.
- The Old Testament shows the ups and downs of the Jewish people and the work of God through the mediation of key figures: patriarchs, kings, priest and prophets.
- Christians believe that Jesus combined all these roles in his life and death, while also being God in human form. Each key figure in the Old Testament gives a glimpse into what Jesus will offer the world.
- In the New Testament, the Bible shows the good news of Jesus working its way through the world as it begins to spread and this reveals how God can work in the life of the Church.
- It is clear throughout the Bible that God speaks to his people directly, through visions and the work of key figures.

Christians believe that the Bible contains God's revelation in some way. Different Christians interpret the Bible differently – either as the Word of God that cannot be wrong or as an inspired text that still holds authority even if it is just an account of how God has worked through the lives of different people.

Now test yourself

TESTED

4 Why is grace so important to revealed theology?
5 What does Calvin say about the centrality to faith of God's revelation through Jesus?

Strengths

- Only God can properly reveal something as indescribable as himself – compare the idea of religious experiences which often emphasise how indescribable it is to encounter God directly.
- The concept of faith reflects the difference when talking about knowing things on earth and knowing God, so revealed theology must be required to know about God.
- The concept of grace shows how humans need to appreciate that God is so much greater than them and they require his revelation to know about him.
- Revealed theology emphasises the special nature of Jesus and gives appropriate importance to Jesus.
- Understanding the Bible as a revealed text shows how God has left that revelation for all to have access to.

Weaknesses

- The idea of revealed theology is of no use to the non-believer because they cannot interpret or understand it.

- Revealed theology suggests a God who only reveals himself in certain circumstances and so could be accused of being biased in some way to some people.
- People who claim that God has revealed himself in some way have contradicted others who claim that God has revealed himself to them.
- Revealed theology does not always make it clear how humans are to interpret what is revealed to them.
- Revealed theology assumes that Christianity is the correct revelation.

Revision activity

For each of these strengths and weaknesses, give them a score out of 5 depending on how good a point they are.

3.4 Has the Fall completely removed all natural human knowledge of God?

REVISED

Calvin's views about natural theology have been explored by theologians: it is not always clear if he agreed with the usefulness of natural theology. Some of this uncertainty is highlighted in the debate between the Swiss theologians Emil Brunner and Karl Barth, who both come from the Calvinist Reformed tradition. Essentially, the question is whether the Fall has blocked humans' ability to recognise the point of contact between God and humans.

Making links

Your work in Chapter 1, Augustine's teaching on human nature, will overlap with this issue.

Brunner	Barth
It is possible for us to know God through natural theology – the conscience and the *sensus divinitas*	God is so 'radically other' that we cannot use reason to know God – like pouring the Niagara Falls into a milk jug
Humans recognise the point of contact between God and themselves and then become aware of their own sinfulness	Human language came about to describe human things so we can never fully describe God or the human relationship to him
Natural theology cannot save people – however, it can create a discussion that points towards the existence of God	Human reason cannot be fully trusted – we must not put ourselves in a position where we put reason above God
Natural theology can help us to be aware that there is a God, but there is a limit to what we can know	The Bible contains God's revelation but it is only 'God's Word' because God allows revelation to occur through it
The Fall damaged people on some levels, but could not affect the spiritual level, which means there is still a way we can connect to God	Human nature was completely corrupted by the Fall so only through revelation can God interact with humanity

Whereas Barth would have said that he was trying to get to the heart of what Calvin and the Reformers were trying to teach, some have accused him of having been too scared of the rise of Nazism. His view was that if reason had allowed the Nazi party to take power, how could reason ever be useful?

Barth's point is that with our limited ability to understand big ideas and with the effects of the Fall, any attempt to use reason will end up with us misunderstanding God. However, rather than being defeatist, Barth was also clear that we do not need natural theology because God has fully revealed all we need to know in salvation history and ultimately in Jesus. Barth can be countered by the idea that the Bible points us in the direction of natural theology and Barth himself believed that the Bible was revealed by God, so the Bible must be telling us to use natural theology.

Exam tip

Make sure you focus on what Barth and Brunner were saying about natural theology and its relevance.

Now test yourself

TESTED

6 What did each of Brunner and Barth say about the Fall's influence on natural theology?

3.5 Is belief in God's existence sufficient to put one's trust in him?

Christians put a great deal of weight on the idea of faith, but it is important to ask if faith can ever be a sufficient (good enough) reason to believe that God exists. In order to explore this, it is important to understand what a believer thinks faith is: it is the ability to let go of rational thought to put complete trust in God. Often, the evidence for having faith is a feeling that is in itself indescribable and that is logically private to that individual.

Some people think that faith can be tested to be genuine through the lifestyle of a person. Someone with true faith will live a life that tries to be different from the norm; someone who has found faith is likely to change the way they live. However, this could be said only to prove that they believe their faith is real, rather than the fact that their faith points to God.

Thinkers, such as Richard Dawkins, reject faith on the grounds that it is filling in the gaps where perhaps we simply do not currently know the answers to big questions. Dawkins champions the view that science will be able to answer key questions of theology and philosophy at some point.

In the book of *Acts*, Paul encounters the thinkers of Athens and explains to them that their altar 'to an unknown God' demonstrates that they worship the Christian God without knowing it (*Acts* 17:23). This passage can be used to support the idea of natural theology because it suggests that there is a point of contact – a *sensus divinitas* – from which conclusions about God can be gained using reason. It also calls into question what faith is: do we need to know exactly what we are believing in to have 'true' faith? Does it matter whether or not we have faith in the specifically Christian God? This overlaps with the work on election in Chapter 2, Death and the afterlife, and religious pluralism in Chapter 7.

However, further on in the chapter, Paul talks about a crunch moment in history where, because of Jesus, humans need to be aware of what they are worshipping. This seems to suggest that there is a need for revealed theology as well as – or perhaps instead of – natural theology.

Other people would point to wider evidence. There are many challenges to belief, such as the problem of evil, modern science and the rise of secularism. Christians would have responses to each of these, but would also say that it is important not to put too much emphasis on things that come from the mind because God's revelation of himself is more pure than the human tendency to over-think might suggest. We must continue to remember that God is very different to other things we might use our reason to (try to) understand.

> **Key quote**
>
> Faith is the great cop-out, the great excuse to evade the need to think and evaluate evidence. Faith is belief in spite of, even perhaps because of, the lack of evidence.
>
> Richard Dawkins, from a speech at the Edinburgh International Science Festival, 15 April 1992

> **Key quote**
>
> He has given proof of this to everyone by raising him from the dead.
>
> *Acts* 17:31

> **Making links**
>
> The problem of evil is explored in the Philosophy of Religion book, Chapter 6.
>
> Secularism is explored in Chapter 9, The challenge of secularism.

Now test yourself

7 How did Richard Dawkins describe faith?
8 What was written on the altar in Athens that Paul saw?

3.6 Is natural knowledge of God the same as revealed knowledge of God?

The *Acts* passage about the altar to the unknown God might suggest that the distinction between natural and revealed theology is not as clear as we might think. One question to ask is whether the type of knowledge we gain from each is the same. Is it possible to say that we know God personally through natural theology? Is personal knowledge better than other types of knowledge or is it more subjective? Scientific knowledge is very important, but the way that a poet understands the world is surely just as relevant.

It is possible to suggest that natural and revealed theology are very similar because the points of contact in natural theology are there since God has decided they should be there: on some level, God has revealed it. For example, some people see the conscience not as an argument for natural theology but as a revelation from God.

Equally, when looking at the Bible as a type of revelation, it could be said that reason is required to find the authentic message within it, so, just like Aquinas argued, revelation can come from reason. The Bible also celebrates human reason and many people associate the 'likeness' that God created humans in as referring to human intelligence. If God created us with rationality, then perhaps from the creator's point of view there is less distinction between natural and revealed theology than we might think.

Ultimately, there are some Christian beliefs that cannot be understood through natural theology – for example, the Trinity or the incarnation. This is why Christian theology has always come back to the importance of revelation in the world with the underlying assumption that revealed theology can be fully understood with right reason.

The key difference between the two has to be the process that they use to gain knowledge. In the same way that I may find out about one thing by reading a book and find out about a person by meeting them, I am gaining knowledge in different ways. Equally, I may read a lot about the Prime Minister but when I come to meet him or her then I might come to know different things.

Whether or not they are two sides of the same coin, the same thing by different names or whether natural theology needs to be rejected must be examined using a combination of all the arguments through this chapter.

> **Making links**
>
> See Chapter 8 in the Religion and Ethics book for more on conscience.

> **Key quote**
>
> Let us make mankind in our image, in our likeness.
> *Genesis* 1:26

> **Revision activity**
>
> Make a table with three columns:
> 1 Natural theology is the same as revealed theology.
> 2 Natural theology and revealed theology work together.
> 3 Natural theology should be rejected.
>
> Now add arguments, including key scholars' views, from the whole chapter to each column.

3.7 Summary and exam tips

Exam checklist

- Explain and evaluate natural knowledge of God's existence.
- Explain and evaluate revealed knowledge of God's existence.
- Consider how important the Fall was in removing human ability to know God.
- Consider what makes true faith and how this relates to knowing God.

Sample work

The best paragraphs in essays start with an argument for or against the question and develop from there. Here we imagine an essay asking us to evaluate natural knowledge of God.

First attempt	Improvement
Natural theology states that there is a point of contact between God and the earth in some way, such as in the beauty of the world.	Natural theology seems to explain the sense of awe we have when we consider the beauty of the world. This is an example of a point of contact between God and the world which is the starting point for natural theology. From this point of contact, we use our reason to lead us to conclusions about God and God's existence.

Going further: Interpreting the Bible

It is useful background information to understand that most scholars do not read the Bible at face value. If you are able to talk (in a number of topics) about different approaches to the Bible, you can show a depth of theological appreciation that will enhance your analysis. In this topic, it will help you explore the extent to which the Bible is direct revelation from God. If it is possible to interpret the Bible in some or all of the ways below, to what extent can the Bible be said to be the Word of God? What is the implication of saying that there are earlier versions of some of the books of the Bible, or of saying that we can see an author's hand at work in the text? If these approaches are rejected, can we really call the Bible a 'text'?

Some of the many different ways of analysing the Bible include:

Source criticism	The idea that when analysing a text, it is possible to explore the sources that different parts of the text come from to learn more about the origins of that text.	The two creation stories in *Genesis* seem to come from different sources – one that calls God 'God' and one that calls God by his name 'YHWH'.
Form criticism	The exploration of why Biblical writers structured their text in specific ways.	Mark's Gospel is fond of the 'sandwich' approach where an important idea is sandwiched between two halves of a story – this serves to emphasise key themes (e.g. *Mark* 5:21–43).
Redaction criticism	The exploration of why writers have edited their original sources in certain ways.	Matthew and Luke, with Mark as an original source, sometimes seem to edit Mark to emphasise themes of interest to them (e.g. the Jewish community to Matthew and women to Luke).

4 The person of Jesus Christ

4.1 Introduction

Jesus is, of course, what makes Christianity distinctive. Jesus took aspects of the Jewish faith and made them his own, attracting followers and starting a movement that soon afterwards began to be known as a separate religion. These followers spoke of the teachings and actions of Jesus but also that his crucifixion by the Romans was not the end of his life, but that he rose from the dead and continued to appear to his followers.

As Christianity spread, the nature of Jesus was explored, challenged and defined carefully. By the year 451, Jesus was acknowledged by mainstream Christianity as fully God and fully human. This made Jesus different to other inspiring preachers and different to other prophets.

Jesus' teachings are perhaps summed up in the way he turned the society he lived in upside down: he spoke of a God of love, not punishment, and a God who welcomes everyone, even outcasts. In some ways, it could be argued that Jesus was more of a prophet than anything else, but he was certainly a teacher and some might argue a teacher of wisdom. His work with outcasts and the poor makes some consider him a liberator.

In modern theology, the quest for the historical Jesus was very important during the twentieth century. This quest aimed to find out who the Jesus of history was and how similar he was to the Jesus portrayed in the Gospels. This quest also asked questions about who Jesus thought he was and whether he thought his relationship with God was similar to, or different from, other people's.

> **Key quote**
>
> The Self-same Perfect in Godhead, the Self-same Perfect in Manhood; truly God and truly Man ... co-essential with the Father according to the Godhead, the Self-same co-essential with us according to the Manhood.
>
> *Chalcedonian Definition of Jesus Christ*, Council of Chalcedon, 451

> **Now test yourself**
>
> 1 Fill in the gaps: Jesus is believed by Christians to be fully _____ and fully _____.
>
> TESTED

The specification says

Topic	Content	Key knowledge
The person of Jesus Christ	● Jesus Christ's authority as: – the Son of God	● Jesus' divinity as expressed in his: – knowledge of God – miracles – resurrection With reference to *Mark* 6:47–52 and *John* 9:1–41
	– a teacher of wisdom	● Jesus' moral teaching on: – repentance and forgiveness – inner purity and moral motivation With reference to *Matthew* 5:17–48 and *Luke* 15:11–32
	– a liberator	● Jesus' role as liberator of the marginalised and the poor, as expressed in his: – challenge to political authority – challenge to religious authority With reference to *Mark* 5:24–34 and *Luke* 10:25-37
Learners should have the opportunity to discuss issues related to Christian ideas regarding Jesus Christ as a source of authority, including: ● whether or not Jesus was only a teacher of wisdom ● whether or not Jesus was more than a political liberator ● whether or not Jesus' relationship with God was very special or truly unique ● whether or not Jesus thought he was divine.		

4.2 Jesus the Son of God

The phrase 'Son of God' meant different things to Jews and Gentiles at the time of Jesus. For Jews, it tended to mean someone specially chosen by God, perhaps with angelic or supernatural aspects. For Gentiles, it was a way of saying someone was divine. For Jesus to be known as Son of God in the New Testament was a way of saying all of this at once to both audiences.

The special nature of his conception and birth seem to show Jesus as being very literally the Son of God. At his baptism and transfiguration, God specifically calls Jesus his son, but Jesus does not seem to use the title of himself. Some think that this was because the idea of him being divine was written into the texts later, whereas others think that this is because Jesus did not want to attract unnecessary attention from the religious authorities.

Jesus' knowledge of God

Jesus calls God 'Abba' or Dad but spends time in prayer. It seems from some of the Gospel accounts that he did not see himself as equal to God. In John's Gospel, there are a number of sayings of Jesus that begin 'I am', written in Greek in the same way that the Greek version of the Old Testament referred to the unspoken name of God. This seems to be a clear indication that Jesus was referring to himself as God, although some point out that John's Gospel was written a long time after the other Gospels and so the point may have been John's own addition to the Jesus story to match the theology of early Christianity, rather than reflecting historical truth.

Miracles

Jesus' miracles seem to suggest that he had God's power in a special way. The New Testament talks of miracles as works of power and great wonder. John's Gospel uses the word for a 'sign' to describe the miracles, suggesting that these are signs that point to Jesus' **divinity**. Magicians were commonplace at the time of Jesus and some think that on their own miracles do not specifically show Jesus to be divine. Unlike the magicians, however, Jesus did not perform miracles as tricks to make people believe – after his miracles he often asked people not to talk about what had happened. Also, miracles such as the calming of the sea showed Jesus performing actions that only God was thought to be able to do, which points further to Jesus' divinity.

> **Key word**
>
> **Divinity** The divine aspect of Jesus – the part of Jesus that is God

Resurrection

Jesus' resurrection was enough proof for the disciples of the truth behind Jesus' message and authority that they began a new religious movement. The Gospels make an effort to show Jesus as having really died and really been buried (for example, the spear piercing his side and blood flowing out), only for that tomb to be found empty with the grave clothes discarded. Paul's letters, written before the Gospels, speak of Jesus' appearances to his followers but not the empty tomb, making some thinkers suggest that the resurrection should not be taken literally.

However, the literal truth of the resurrection event is central to Christian belief. The emphasis is that Jesus, as God, raised himself from the dead to show that, for humans, death is not the end. It is the ultimate sign for Christians that Jesus came to earth both as human and divine: he died but broke through that barrier and therefore is a special intermediary between God and humans; he knows what it is to be human but also shows that God is completely in control. As Paul said in 1 *Corinthians* 15:17, 'if Christ has not been raised, your faith is futile; you are still in your sins'.

Key texts

- In *Mark* 6:47–52, Jesus walks on water – a miracle story that helps the disciples to understand what they had previously witnessed when he fed the 5000. When Jesus identifies himself to the disciples he uses the special 'I am' phrase to help them understand: Jesus' power comes from his identity as God.
- In *John* 9:1–41, Jesus first performs a miracle, healing a blind man. This convinces the man that Jesus' power comes from God, but the authorities do not accept this. Jesus uses this event to explain to the authorities that it is not just physical blindness that he is here to heal, but spiritual blindness – the blindness that makes them not realise who they are dealing with.

> **Exam tip**
>
> It is important when discussing evidence in the Bible not just to write out Bible stories. You need to analyse them and relate them to the question set in the essay.

> **Revision activity**
>
> In order of strength of evidence, make a list of evidence that Jesus was Son of God. Try to explain why you have placed them in that order.

Now test yourself
TESTED

2 How did Jesus differ from the magicians of his day?
3 What special name does Jesus use to speak to God the Father?

4.3 Jesus as a teacher of wisdom
REVISED

Jesus' sayings were often similar to those in the book of *Proverbs*, one of the examples of wisdom literature (books that tend to be a series of challenging statements that teach about God and life) in the Old Testament, and his one-liners gave insight and were memorable to those who heard them. Jesus' parables were stories that were designed to catch the attention of his contemporaries and to think differently about the world around them.

In Christianity, Jesus' wisdom comes from the fact that he is God as well as human. His experience of the world is completely different to ours. Some argue that encounters with heaven such as at his baptism or transfiguration might have given him the wisdom that he communicated in his teaching, but for others, this direct access to God would be more of a sign that he was not human, simply divine.

Jesus, in challenging the Judaism of his day, wanted people to take responsibility for their actions but to get their priorities right: for example, he said that the Sabbath was made for humans, not the other way around – the Sabbath Law needed to be kept in perspective. Religion and morality help humans get to God – purity is about what is on the inside, not what rituals are being followed.

Teachings on repentance and forgiveness, inner purity and morality

A theme in Jesus' teachings was **repentance** and **forgiveness**. Jesus praised the repentance of Zacchaeus the tax collector or those of his disciples who left behind old lives to follow him.

Indeed, Jesus taught that people should not forgive an action just once or just seven times, but seventy times seven times – a light-hearted way of telling people that forgiveness should be a constant thing, not a one-off event. The prayer Jesus left the Church, the 'Our Father', places forgiveness at the centre of daily prayer for the Christian when it says, 'forgive us our trespasses (sins) as we forgive those who trespass (sin) against us'.

Key words

Repent To turn your life in a new direction, away from your past life

Forgive To let go of past anger and move on in life

Now test yourself

TESTED

4 When did Jesus have special encounters with heaven?
5 Which key Jewish Law did Jesus say needed to be kept in perspective?

Key texts

Matthew 5:17–48 is towards the beginning of the Sermon on the Mount. It is a series of teachings of Jesus, apparently given while he was on a mountain, surrounded by crowds. Some think it is similar in content and approach to wisdom literature. The moral teachings put the accountability onto the believer, not onto religious practices. It is important to seek inner purity and to have correct moral motivation.

Section of passage	Meaning	Interpretation
Teaching about the law	Jesus has come to fulfil the law, not to replace it. Christians need to be more faithful than the teachers of the law.	Christians must not pick and choose their interpretation of the law and all people are responsible for moral decisions, not just the teachers of the law.
Teaching about anger	Whoever is angry needs to make peace with their brother as being angry is as bad as the murder that it can lead to.	Christians might strive for harmony in all aspects of their lives – and repent to bring about that harmony.
Teaching about adultery	Whoever thinks lustfully about a woman has committed adultery in his heart – it is better to cut off parts of your body that cause you to sin than for your whole body to go to hell.	The Christian must be pure in their thoughts, as well as their deeds – both are as important as the other.
Teaching about divorce	Divorce, which used to be allowed for many reasons, is now to be very rare.	The Christian way does not have easy ways out of difficult situations.
Teaching about vows	Don't swear by oaths – just let Yes mean Yes and No mean No	There should be no hidden agenda for the Christian; personal integrity is key.
Teaching about revenge and enemies	Turn the other cheek – go the extra mile – love your enemies	Christians must always strive to be the 'bigger people' in a situation.

Making links

How does this link to your study of situation ethics (see Religion and Ethics book, Chapter 2)?

Luke 15:11–32 is known as the parable of the lost son. A man's younger son asks for his inheritance early (essentially telling his father that he wishes he were dead), wastes the money and then comes to the realisation that he had done wrong and decides to return to his father. Jesus shows through the story the process of realising you have done wrong, turning your life around (repentance) and being forgiven. While the focus is on the sinner, the younger son, it is clear that God's forgiveness is total: the father runs and embraces his son even before the son has said the word 'sorry'. The idea seems to be that nothing is bad enough for God not to forgive if a person repents. The wisdom that Jesus is teaching in this passage seems to be that God's love and forgiveness is huge, but humans need to remember that they are responsible for their actions and need to repent.

> **Key quote**
>
> Be perfect, therefore, as your heavenly father is perfect.
>
> *Matthew 5:48*

> **Exam tip**
>
> You need to be able to know which of the key text passages is which by the chapter and verse numbers.

> **Revision activity**
>
> Review the text of *Matthew* 5:17–48 and make a spider diagram highlighting the key features of the passage.

Now test yourself

TESTED ☐

6 Which set passage talks about inner purity and correct moral motivation?
7 What does *Luke* 15:11–32 teach about God's forgiveness?

4.4 Jesus as a liberator

REVISED ☐

Luke's birth stories about Jesus suggest that he would have a special relationship with the poor and marginalised. In these stories the baby Jesus was placed in a feeding trough as a crib and his first visitors were the semi-outcast shepherds. In Matthew's Gospel, the wise men make King Herod feel challenged by a potential threat to his power. Religion and politics were closely linked in first-century Israel and there are overlaps between those in political authority and those in religious authority.

> **Key word**
>
> **Liberator** Someone who frees a person or group of people

Challenge to political authority

Jesus clashed with the politicians of his day on many occasions.

- He talked about the Kingdom of God – a political statement because it suggested that authority was going to be taken away from those with earthly authority.
- He made tax collectors, who represented the government, turn away from their former lifestyles and follow him.
- In the last week of his life, he:
  - publicly entered Jerusalem on a peaceful donkey, not a military horse, suggesting he would bring about peace where the government could not
  - turned over the tables in the temple, objecting to the fact it had lost its religious focus
  - was crucified by the Roman government as a trouble-maker.

Challenge to religious authority

- Jesus was accused of not following the strict laws relating to the Sabbath, but he said that following the laws needed to be kept in perspective.
- Jesus was criticised for eating with outcasts, but he said that he was here to help those people who needed him most.
- Jesus was said not to respect the purification laws, but he pointed out that following rules is not the same as worshipping God properly.
- The religious authorities objected to Jesus forgiving sins because only God could forgive sins.

Jesus the liberator

Jesus certainly inspired those who are seen as the underdogs of society. The liberation he brought seems to have been less about upsetting and reforming the authorities and more about preparing people for the new kingdom – the one where God is in charge. The liberation Jesus brought was liberation from spiritual states as much as physical states and applied to all sectors of society, including those from other countries.

Key texts

	Mark 5:24–34 – The woman with the flow of blood	*Luke* 10:25–37 – The parable of the Good Samaritan
Outline	The woman who had been bleeding for 12 years would have been an outcast from society because she could not have taken part in synagogue worship as the blood would have made her ritually unclean according to the law.	Before the famous parable, Jesus encourages the teacher of the law to follow the law in the scriptures.
Analysis	Her faith causes her healing.	The Samaritans were not trusted by Jews because of historic issues. They were seen as traitors who had let down the Jewish people.
How this is liberation	Her interaction with Jesus makes her liberated from the spiritual aspects of her illness – from being an outcast.	Not only does the Samaritan set an example of how to be a neighbour but the parable teaches that people must be neighbours to everyone, whoever they are. Jesus teaches that all are equal and so all people are liberated by him.

Now test yourself

TESTED

8 Why did the authorities feel challenged when Jesus forgave sins?
9 Why was the woman in *Mark* 5:24–34 an outcast?

Revision activity

Make a list of other passages or stories about Jesus that you studied in class that show Jesus as being a liberator for the marginalised and poor.

4.5 Discussing the issues

Was Jesus only a teacher of wisdom?

Much of Jesus' ministry was made up of him teaching, through sayings, through parables and through the example of miracles. Some suggest that his main aim was to purify Judaism, rather than to start a new religious movement: he seemed to expect the new Kingdom to come quickly and most of his work was with the Jewish people around him, rather than the Gentiles as well.

Some modern scholars have tried to strip away the elements of the Gospel that are likely to have sprung up after the time of Jesus and, in removing the supernatural elements, we are left with a teacher of wisdom. Some people find it difficult to accept that Jesus was divine, especially as there is little evidence that Jesus taught this about himself.

Jesus' teaching was certainly authentic – it engaged people on a new level and made people think about the situation that they lived in, but some would argue that this does not mean he was 'only' a teacher of wisdom: they would say that it is the whole picture – the miracle worker who rose from the dead – that gave Jesus particular authority.

Jesus also started new systems that would last beyond his time on earth, such as the Eucharist, and he saw himself as having followers who would carry on his work. He also taught his followers how to pray, suggesting that they would need to be in it for the long haul.

Was Jesus more than a political liberator?

There is certainly a great deal of material that suggests that Jesus' challenges to the authorities of his time were significant. Jesus thought that people had got too bogged down with following the letter of the law, rather than trying to understand the thinking behind it. He came as a champion of all people into a country occupied by the Romans. However, there are several arguments that suggest that political liberation was not the prime focus for Jesus.

> **Key quote**
> Give back to Caesar what is Caesar's and to God what is God's.
> *Mark* 12:17

- Jesus told his followers to pay taxes and Paul also echoed this view that Christians need to be lawful citizens.
- Jesus escaped when he realised that people would try to make him king by force (*John* 6:15).
- He did not resist arrest by the guards when he could have done – and he stopped his followers from using violence.
- He seems not to have agreed with the political views of the zealots who wanted to overthrow the Romans – for example, he rode into Jerusalem not on a military horse, but on a donkey.
- He seems mainly concerned with inner purity rather than outward shows of force.
- Jesus said that he had not come to abolish the law or the prophets (the Jewish tradition), but to fulfil them. He was trying to develop people's understanding, not replace it.
- The emphasis on the marginalised is particularly evident in Luke's Gospel and some scholars think that this was editing done by Luke to make Jesus more relevant for his particular audience.

Was Jesus' relationship with God very special or truly unique?

Jesus was known to speak with authority and he certainly had at least a special relationship with God, giving him the confidence to teach within the context of his time. As a teacher of wisdom, prophet and liberator, he sits in the tradition of many Old Testament figures who had special relationships with God. Jesus modelled an excellent religious lifestyle, taking time to pray, always remembering God was at the centre of the decisions people make and perhaps understanding that religion needs to be reinterpreted for each new situation. As a miracle worker, he was certainly special, even raising people from the dead; but even in the Old Testament there are examples of people being brought back to life.

However, it seems from the Gospels that there was more to Jesus than this. His miraculous birth, surrounded by unusual visitors, a moment of religious experience at his baptism and then again at his transfiguration and his resurrection from death by crucifixion all seem to suggest that Jesus was more than just another prophet. Jesus seemed to embody both the Jewish and Gentile understandings of what it meant to be a Son of God.

In the modern quest for the historical Jesus, even where many of the stories might be understood as inventions by the Gospel writers, there remains a basic tradition of Jesus being a miracle worker and inspirational teacher. The resurrection, however, is a key moment that changes our understanding of everything that has gone before.

Did Jesus think he was divine?

It is difficult to understand how Jesus could have been completely God and completely human. From our perspective, it seems that if he was aware of being one then he could not have been aware of being the other. Many Christians would explain this by suggesting that the nature of knowledge is different for God than it is for us.

Christians believe that Jesus did not just exist when he was born, but that he is an eternal part of the Trinity – God as Father, Son and Holy Spirit. Jesus, therefore, existed before the universe was created. In *John 8:58*, Jesus states clearly that he existed before Abraham, once more using the special 'I am' phrase. Even as a child, Jesus showed wisdom beyond his years when, having been lost by his parents, he said to them, 'Didn't you know I had to be in my Father's house?'

Jesus certainly experienced emotions and had moments where he felt abandoned by God. He was also very aware of his mission from God to intervene in the world in a unique way. It may be that this sense of mission helped him to focus more on his human nature while he was on earth. At the very least, this shows immense trust in God, but perhaps this was a trust founded in the knowledge that everything was part of a plan for the salvation of the world that had been in place since the Fall.

> **Making links**
>
> The nature of divine knowledge is explored in the Philosophy of Religion book, Chapter 7.

> **Revision activity**
>
> To help you with AO2, summarise the evidence in this section and give each point a mark out of 5 for how strong the evidence is. You could also give reasons why you think this point is strong or weak.

> **Typical mistake**
>
> Weaker essays don't focus specifically on the question set. If the question asks about whether Jesus was divine, don't make it into a question on whether Jesus was only a teacher of wisdom, even if you wanted that title to come up!

4.6 Summary and exam tips

> ### Exam checklist
> - Explain the idea of Jesus' divinity as Son of God.
> - Explain evidence that suggests Jesus was a teacher of wisdom.
> - Explain how Jesus liberated the marginalised and the poor.
> - Evaluate who Jesus really was: teacher, liberator, God.
> - Analyse Jesus' knowledge of himself and God.

Sample work

Questions that require you to compare different aspects of a topic can be quite tricky and it is important not to list everything you can think of to do with one aspect, followed by everything from the other aspect! Make sure you combine your analysis with showing off everything you know, but start with analysis and evaluation. Here we are comparing whether Jesus was more of a teacher of wisdom than a liberator.

First attempt	Improvement
Jesus' teachings were full of sayings that people could remember – for example, in his views on forgiveness shown in *Luke* 15:11–32. Jesus also can be seen as a liberator of the marginalised – for example, in his interaction with outcasts.	It could be said that the majority of Jesus' teachings were in line with those of a teacher of wisdom. There are many examples of Jesus using memorable sayings, such as in *Luke* 15:11–32, where he teaches about forgiveness in the story of the lost son, and these can be found throughout the Gospels. However, also found through the Gospels is Jesus' work with outcasts: he includes everyone in the promise of the Kingdom, even Samaritans. Therefore, it seems that Jesus as a teacher of wisdom and Jesus as a liberator are both major strands of his mission.

Going further: Early heresies

Jesus was declared to have been both truly God and truly human in the fourth and fifth centuries, but it took a while for the Church to get there. The first few hundred years of Christianity's history was peppered with heresies (beliefs that go against mainstream or accepted views) that challenged the nature of Jesus. Some are listed below.

- **Docetism** in the second century suggested that Jesus' human side was only a veil that made people think he was human. It was challenged by an emphasis on Jesus' human characteristics, especially his death.
- **Adoptionism**, also in the second century, said that Jesus the human was adopted by God at his baptism, who then left him when he died on the cross as a human. This led to the careful expression by Christianity of belief in the Trinity.
- **Arianism** in the fourth century suggested that God the Son was less important than God the Father, because he was at some point begotten by God the Father. Arianism was challenged by the statement in mainstream Christianity that the Father and the Son were of the same substance.
- **Nestorianism** in the early fifth century said that Jesus was not fully divine. It was condemned by the Church, which wished to uphold Jesus' full divinity.

5 Christian moral principles

5.1 Introduction

REVISED

It could be said that a religion is characterised as much by its **morals** as by its beliefs. There are many approaches to morals within Christianity and this section explores three. Much of your work for the Religion and Ethics paper will support this, especially the topics of natural law and situation ethics.

> **Key word**
>
> **Morals** A set of principles linked to doing right actions

For some Christians, the diversity in approach is to be celebrated, perhaps because the intention to do good could be seen as at least as important as the action itself. However, for others, authoritative factors help us to identify what is right and what is wrong and it is important that these are followed.

In the Roman Catholic tradition, the authority of the words of Jesus, spoken to the apostles and passed down through the Church, holds high authority. For many Protestants, the Bible is the highest authority, with different traditions giving different weight to reason and to Church teachings. For some Christians, what is right and what is wrong is based on one single authority – love.

We can divide these approaches into three:
1 **Theonomous Christian ethics**. These place God at the centre: God's commandments are what is required for living morally. Humans are so sinful because of the Fall that they cannot make right decisions for themselves and so they must use the direct words of God, found in the Bible.
2 **Heteronomous Christian ethics**. There is a variety of sources of authority for morals. The Bible remains important, but, perhaps because it was written so long ago, morality requires additional support to be understood. This support can come from the Church or from reason, or both.
3 **Autonomous Christian ethics**. The authority is placed onto the individual. The idea behind it is that Christian ethics are ethical decisions that happen to be made by Christians; here we look at those ethics that use love as the guiding force that helps Christians make moral decisions.

The specification says

Topic	Content	Key knowledge
Christian moral principles	● The diversity of Christian moral reasoning and practices and sources of ethics, including:	
	– the Bible as the only authority for Christian ethical practices	● As the Bible reveals God's will then only biblical ethical commands must be followed
	– Bible, Church and reason as the sources of Christian ethical practices	● Christian ethics must be a combination of biblical teaching, Church teaching and human reason
	– love (*agape*) as the only Christian ethical principle which governs Christian practices	● Jesus' only command was to love and that human reason must decide how best to apply this
	Learners should have the opportunity to discuss issues related to diversity of Christian moral principles, including: ● whether or not Christian ethics are distinctive ● whether or not Christian ethics are personal or communal ● whether or not the principle of love is sufficient to live a good life ● whether or not the Bible is a comprehensive moral guide.	

Now test yourself

TESTED

1 Which approach to ethics might suggest that the Fall has made humans unable to make moral decisions for themselves?

5.2 The Bible as the only source of ethics

REVISED

A theonomous approach to Christian ethics sees the Bible as containing all a person needs to live a good life. Behind this is the idea that the Bible is a set of truth statements that reveal God's message to the world: it is **propositional revelation**. If the Bible is, indeed, a set of statements that God has made then it is logical that these statements should be followed directly.

Key word

Propositional revelation The idea that God reveals himself in truth statements. To say that the Bible is an example of this is to say that the Bible is a series of truth statements

The Bible itself makes claims that it is to be taken at this level:

All Scripture is God-breathed and is useful for teaching, rebuking, correcting and training in righteousness.

2 Timothy 3:16

You must understand that no prophecy of Scripture came about by the prophet's own interpretation of things. For prophecy never had its origin in the human will, but prophets, though humans, spoke from God.

2 Peter 1:20–21

Some Christians see the Bible not as dictated by God but inspired and still accurate. This approach is borne out by the nature of the Bible: it is full of several different types of text, including stories of people, which need to be understood as holding a message for life today.

For this approach to work, it is important that Christians embrace the whole text of the Bible, rather than choosing some 'favourite' passages. It is also important to recognise that the Bible is interpreted the minute it is read and that this cannot be helped: literalists do allow this approach to interpretation.

Typical mistake

Some candidates suggest that literalist interpretations of the Bible only read the words at face value. However, a literalist in twenty-first century Tanzania will read the words and immediately interpret them very differently to someone in thirteenth-century Italy. It is important not to over-simplify complex issues.

Analysing theonomous ethics

Some suggest the Bible contains contradictions, such as a change in approach to revenge and violence between Old and New Testaments. However, theonomous Christian ethics might argue that the Bible looks at situations from different angles in different places and that much of the Old Testament was replaced by the New Testament. This still leaves the approach open to criticism, however, because it seems that interpretation is required, which could point to the need for the use of reason or Church guidance.

Another criticism is that the Bible contains many different styles of writing and some of these styles are written in a specific context by a person (e.g. the letters of Paul to different Churches). This would suggest that the Bible cannot have been written by one author (God). However, this point could be criticised itself because it seems to limit God to being like a human, able only to write in one way.

A strength of using the Bible as the only source of morality is that it provides clear guidelines that cannot be questioned. However, some would observe that some modern situations are not covered by the Bible and any attempt to apply Biblical content to these situations would be using our reason, which is not true theonomous ethics.

Now test yourself

TESTED

2 What is a propositional statement?
3 Is the idea that the Bible has different styles of writing an argument for or against taking the Bible as the only form of authority in ethics?

5.3 Bible, Church and reason

The Bible has not always existed in its current form. During the second century, Christian leaders gathered together to choose which of the many books around at the time had sufficient authority to make up the New Testament. The key criterion was that of apostolicity: the idea that it must have a direct link to an apostle. The books were arranged in the order we now see them, discarding other Gospels and other letters. For some, this was simply the Church identifying which books were God-breathed, but for others it is a clear example of the Church using its authority to select the authentic tradition of Scripture: more than just the Bible is needed to determine what is right and wrong.

Church authority

There are different approaches to Church authority in Christian denominations, as shown in the following table:

Approach by some Protestants	Approach by Roman Catholics
Over 2000 years, the Church has interpreted the Bible and this interpretation should guide people in their moral lives.	The authority of the Church was given by Jesus to Peter and the apostles and itself already existed when the New Testament was put together.
Churches are often governed by councils or synods that guide people in how to live.	Tradition comes from the spoken tradition given to the apostles and handed down over time. It therefore has the same criterion of apostolicity.
The Church is the bridge between the first century and today and its journey is as important as the journey of the first Christians.	Authentic interpretation of the Bible is one of the jobs of the Church, under the influence of the Holy Spirit.
Preaching is a valid method of interpretation for Christians.	'To the Church belongs the right always and everywhere to announce moral principles.' (*Catechism of the Catholic Church*, 2032)
Prayer and worship are ways in which Christians use Scripture and therefore learn from it.	With this authority comes the assertion that there are moral absolutes: some things are simply wrong or right.
The Bible was written after Christianity had existed for some time and so what was written down was written for the specific context of the authors of the different books.	Humans are weak and sinful and therefore cannot rely on themselves to make moral decisions properly – the Bible and Church are required.

These approaches lead to a number of issues:
- Is it reasonable to suggest that humans cannot effectively live their lives without an authority? Would God have created humans that way?
- The relationship between people and the authority of the Church has created problems in Christianity's past and partly led to the Reformation.
- It is unclear how the Church is able to transmit God's authority on a day-to-day basis – does God reveal himself specifically to Church leaders? Corruption within Churches also suggests that Church leaders are as human as others.
- How do we determine when to take the Bible at face value and when to interpret it through the Church?
- Which situations make a new interpretation of the Bible authentic? Who decides?
- If the journey of Christian tradition is valid, can there be absolute right actions and wrong actions? Does this matter?

Revision activity

Which approach do you find more convincing? Or do you reject both? Make sure you can justify your answer

Now test yourself

4 For a book to be included in the New Testament, to whom must the book link directly to?

TESTED

5.4 Bible, Church and reason (continued)

Using reason

For Roman Catholics, reason can be used to identify what God has revealed. The most important area in ethics is in understanding Natural Law. God has a core understanding for the universe (the Eternal Law) and has revealed some laws through the Bible (the Divine Law). The next tier of law is Natural Law, which are the five primary precepts on which humans try to do good and avoid evil. Finally, secondary rules are made that are human laws that fulfil the primary precepts. These human laws are verified by the Church, but can be worked out through reason.

Catholics also give authority to the **conscience** to help make moral decisions. Thomas Aquinas (1224–1274) said that the conscience was reason being used to work out what is right to do (and therefore identifying the secondary rules of Natural Law). In the nineteenth century, John Henry Newman said that conscience has more authority even than the Pope (i.e. the Church) because having a conscience predates the Church's existence.

Many Protestants would agree with some of these principles: reason is, at the very least, required to help distinguish between correct and incorrect interpretations of the Bible. Reason is required to understand the Bible in an ever-changing world, but it is also important to understand reason as trying to establish what would be in the Bible if it were being written in today's context. To be sure, the world today is significantly different from that of the New Testament. These Protestants believe that the Bible can speak into current situations if appropriately analysed. It is important to understand what the context of the Bible writers was and many Protestant communities emphasise the importance of studying the Bible through Bible study groups, as well as engaging in private reflection and listening to preaching. Ultimately, for Protestants, reason still points back to the Bible, which holds ultimate authority.

Analysing heteronomous ethics

Heteronomous approaches to ethics might suggest that the Bible is a form of **non-propositional revelation**. Any heteronomous approach begs three fundamental questions:
1 What sources are the correct sources of authority? Which Church or which Church leader?
2 Where there is disagreement (especially when the reasoning of two individuals differs), who or what has the ultimate authority? Catholics would say the Church; Protestants would say the Bible – both of which have their own problems.
3 Has the ability of God to reveal himself and to be recognised by faith been undermined?

Making links

Natural Law is covered in detail in the Religion and Ethics book, Chapter 1.

Key word

Conscience The inner sense of right and wrong in a person, sometimes described as an internal voice

Key quote

Conscience is a judgement of reason whereby the human person recognises the moral quality of a concrete act that he is going to perform.
Catechism of the Catholic Church, 1778

Revision activity

Make a mind map or other visual note of the information in this section on using reason.

Key word

Non-propositional revelation The idea that God does not reveal himself through truth statements, so the revelation might need interpretation

---

Now test yourself

5 Who said that the conscience is reason working out the right thing to do?

5.5 Love as the only ethical principle

In *Mark* 12:30–31, Jesus summarises all the law as being about love. This is clearly a theme throughout the Gospels and so a starting point for many Christian approaches to ethics. The Greek word for love in this context is **agape**, which is used of the unconditional love that God has for humans and which humans need to try to have for God and the world.

The Bible further clarifies the idea of *agape* as being:
- sacrificial love for others, in the same way that Jesus sacrificed his life
- making yourself a servant
- directed towards everyone, including enemies and outcasts
- eternal.

Paul Tillich (1886–1965) saw love as a central precept, underpinned by justice and growing out of the wisdom of the past. The laws of the Bible are wisdom from which we learn, but central to our ethical decision making needs to be an ultimate fairness for all, which is characterised by love. Tillich rejected non-autonomous approaches to ethics.

Adapting Tillich's thinking, Joseph Fletcher (1905–1991) used this principle of love to determine his theory of situation ethics. In situation ethics, love is the central principle that prevents the Christian from falling into over-reliance on laws or a life without rules. It tells Christians to follow the rules unless it is more loving to do otherwise – to transform a situation into one of love. Fletcher argued that his theory was person-centred, just like Jesus was.

The argument goes that Jesus' Sermon on the Mount was not a replacement for the Ten Commandments, or the whole Jewish Law but a set of illustrations of how to put love into practice. J.A.T. Robinson (1919–1983) described love as having a 'built-in moral compass' which can direct people to the most important need when required – we should trust love.

> **Key word**
>
> *Agape* The unconditional love God has for humans that humans need to try to reflect

> **Making links**
>
> Situation ethics is covered in full detail in the Religion and Ethics book, Chapter 2.

> **Exam tip**
>
> One word can make all the difference – sufficient means 'enough on its own' and so this is not the same as asking if love is important in living a good life.

Analysing autonomous ethics: is love sufficient to live a good life?

Yes	No
Love gives us all we need to have the confidence to follow our instincts.	It is over-simplistic to suggest that Jesus' teachings were only about love.
Love is the only force that can fully recognise the ever-changing moral situations we find ourselves in.	In the same situation, different people might interpret love in different ways.
Love is a fundamental and extreme human emotion and so God could well have expected that to drive us.	Love requires at least reason alongside it to understand how to live life. It is too complicated to be the solution on its own.
Love can empower the Christian to be able to put people first in challenging times, especially when mainstream society needs to be challenged.	Love can become an excuse for people simply doing whatever they want.
Jesus kept returning to the theme of love and so situation ethics seems to reflect his approach. Jesus' authority cannot be denied for Christians.	Agape love is not achievable for most humans. It is unlikely that God would expect the unachievable from his people.

Now test yourself

6 What Greek word means 'unconditional love, like that God has for us'?
7 Which scholar came up with the theory of situation ethics?

5.6 Christian ethics: distinctive, personal, communal

Are Christian ethics distinctive?

Christianity is underpinned by belief in the **incarnation** and resurrection, which means that it is coming from a distinctive starting point from other religions: God reached down to humans, rather than humans needing to reach up towards God. The emphasis on Jesus Christ also leads to the idea for some Christians that personal faith and grace are the primary ways to get to heaven. If this is true, then Christian morals might come less from a central teaching authority than in other communities.

Christians who take a theonomous approach to ethics will have plenty in common with **deontological** forms of ethics, although the emphasis on the Bible will be different. There will also be overlap with Judaism and Islam. Heteronomous approaches, in allowing reason to play a role, have more in common with many of the ethical theories you have studied, although some forms of utilitarianism might overlap more with autonomous approaches, as would situation ethics. Eastern religions have a range of approaches to ethics, which tend to use a combination of sources of authority to help an individual make decisions.

For those Christians who take the Bible literally, their ethical approach might be very different. Using love as a guiding principle also seems distinctive, but it could be argued that love is the same idea as the way that many people approach ethics.

Christianity calls people to be counter-cultural (to challenge society when it loses its way) and to be prophets in the world, such as in the command to love enemies; perhaps on this level Christians can be identified the most as distinctive.

> **Key words**
>
> **Incarnation** God becoming a human being in Jesus Christ
>
> **Deontological** Duty-based approaches to ethics

> **Making links**
>
> Dietrich Bonhoeffer (see Chapter 6) explored the idea of ethics being communal in some detail.

Personal or communal?

The Christian community is both a living community of Christians now and a communal group that stretches back over about 2000 years. The Bible is the story of those early communities, Jewish and Christian; perhaps Christian ethics is about a community expressing moral actions, more than an individual doing them. The idea of Christians building the Kingdom of God is one of building a community, but equally, a community is made up of individuals. In the thinking of Natural Law, ethics is personal but has the ultimate intention of the overall good of society, which reinforces this point from a Catholic perspective.

> **Now test yourself**
>
> 8 What relationship do Christians try to have with the world?
> 9 Does the use of reason suggest Christian ethics is personal or communal?
>
> TESTED

Personal	Communal
The Bible and Church teachings give individuals a way to live life according to their own needs.	The Bible needs to be read as the expression of how a community lives its life.
Jesus spoke to individual circumstances – for example, the woman with the flow of blood.	Jesus spoke to groups more than to individuals, such as in the Sermon on the Mount.
Some Christians apply reason on an individual level to circumstances.	For some Christians, the Bible should be shared and studied in group situations.
The community focus is about worship and prayer, rather than ethics.	Communities work by rules being used and the rules found in the Bible are for the community.
Situation ethics places the emphasis on the individual's ethical decision-making.	Any interpretation of the Bible is done so in a community context – interpretations have changed over time with different communities.

Exam checklist

- Explain the views of Christians who think the Bible is the only authority for ethics.
- Explain the role of reason in the ethics of some Christians.
- Explain the authority of the Church and Church tradition for some Christians.
- Explain *agape* as a possible approach to ethics.
- Evaluate whether Christian ethics are distinctive or special in some way.
- Evaluate whether Christian ethics are about individuals or communities working for moral lives.
- Assess how useful the principle of love is in living a good life.
- Compare the Bible, Church and reason as approaches to ethics.

Sample work

Much is made of essay introductions, but these do not have to be tricky. It's important to use that first paragraph to drive your essay forward.

First attempt	Improvement
In this essay, I am going to discuss whether Christian ethics should come from the Bible or from love alone. This has been an issue that has perplexed scholars for many years.	The Bible is seen by many Christians as the Word of God but one of the key messages of Jesus is that of love and this comes through many of his teachings. It could be argued that love is Jesus' replacement for the Biblical law, or alternatively, that love is simply a convenient summary of what the spirit of the law is about.

Going further: Christian virtue ethics

The pre-Christian Aristotle said that an approach to ethics that was based on making sure you were constantly developing your character (through virtues) was more important than being focused on rules and laws. A virtuous person is reflective and sees life as a constant journey towards the goal of fulfilling one's purpose. Virtue ethics has seen a resurgence in modern times through the work of scholars like Alasdair MacIntyre: we should form habits by imitating role models and thus become people who are able to make good judgements.

Some might argue that this is how Jesus intended his teachings to be taken. Jesus could be said to have wanted to form people into 'good Christians' who were then able to tackle whatever life threw at them.

In the thirteenth century, Thomas Aquinas saw virtues as being interconnected with rules. He did not see rules as being able to be formed in advance for all situations and he felt that being virtuous can help our decision-making.

Christians sometimes list seven specific virtues, which are very similar to key virtues listed by other religions (which might also be an argument against Christian ethics being distinctive):

- Prudence (wisdom)
- Justice (fairness)
- Temperance (self-control)
- Courage (inner strength)
- Faith (in God's revelation)
- Hope (not giving up)
- Love (*agape*)

Starting Christian ethics with an understanding of virtue theory could lead to some interesting answers to the questions raised by this topic:

- It could explain why some Christians believe it is possible by faith alone to get to heaven because true faith requires these virtues (and morality then follows naturally).
- It could explain why Christians who use the Bible alone can have all the tools needed in their lives for ethical living.
- It could solve the question of whether ethics are both personal and communal because an individual might practise the virtues and develop them alongside the community.
- It could unpack the idea of what *agape* means and involves.

Revision activity

If you want to explore this further, make sure that you research Christian approaches to virtue ethics, rather than the theory in general. It's good practice when revising to challenge your brain with wider reading from time to time.

---

6 Christian moral action

6.1 Introduction

REVISED

Dietrich Bonhoeffer (1906–1945) used his experiences with the rise of Nazism from 1933 to explore how Christian life can be fully expressed. His Christianity was radical and re-examined the relationship between Church and State; Bonhoeffer did not think that the Church should always see itself as working with the State, as the tradition in Germany was at the time. Influenced by his experiences in the United States, he felt that the Church needed to understand itself as separate to countries or races. As he began to challenge Hitler's influence, he left behind his pacifist views, realising that Christians could not stand back and let terrible things happen in the world. He was eventually executed for his role in a Resistance attempt to kill Hitler, as well as his consistent teaching against the Nazi ideology.

Throughout his life, Bonhoeffer held firm to three key theological principles, which are very much of the same tradition as Barth:
1 The Wholly Other God is revealed fully in Jesus.
2 Jesus is also fully human and is 'for us'.
3 Humans are social beings and the best expression of this is found in the communal life of the Church.

The third point can be expanded to explore Bonhoeffer's ethics, because it is in community that his ethics take meaning. Bonhoeffer believed that action was at the centre of ethical practice for Christians. This action comes from a Christian's awareness of his or her conscience, which identifies what is right and what is wrong. Bonhoeffer would have rejected Joseph Fletcher's approach to love because first, it is through community, not individual decision-making, that Christians 'do' ethics, and second, love is understood through an understanding of the ultimate leader, Jesus Christ, who is the revelation of God.

Making links

Fletcher's situation ethics is discussed in the Religion and Ethics book, Chapter 2.

The idea of whether Christian approaches to ethics are communal is discussed in Chapter 5, Christian moral principles.

Now test yourself

1 Why is the idea of community so important to Bonhoeffer?

TESTED

The specification says

Topic	Content	Key knowledge
Christian moral action	● The teaching and example of Dietrich Bonhoeffer on:	● Bonhoeffer's teaching on the relationship of Church and State, including:
	– duty to God and duty to the State	– obedience, leadership and doing God's will – justification of civil disobedience
	– Church as community and source of spiritual discipline	● Bonhoeffer's role in the Confessing Church and his own religious community at Finkenwalde
	– the cost of discipleship	● Bonhoeffer's teaching on ethics and action, including: – 'costly grace' – sacrifice and suffering – solidarity

Topic	Content	Key knowledge
Christian moral action	Learners should have the opportunity to discuss issues related to Christian moral action in the life and teaching of Bonhoeffer, including: ● whether or not Christians should practise civil disobedience ● whether or not it is possible always to know God's will ● whether or not Bonhoeffer puts too much emphasis on suffering ● whether or not Bonhoeffer's theology has relevance today.	

6.2 Duty to God and duty to the State

German Christianity was split in the 1930s. Some Christians, believing that the State's laws were an expression of God's laws, linked with the Nazi ideology and became a part of the official German Church: Hitler was 'inspired' by the Holy Spirit. Anyone with Jewish ancestry was banned from Church office. Others wished to break away from politics entirely and were members of the Confessing Church, named because they believed that they were the only Christians who were truly 'confessing' their faith.

Bonhoeffer's experiences in America gave him a global perspective on what Christianity is. He moved to America briefly in 1939 because he wanted to avoid being made to serve in Hitler's army, but he realised that this was hypocritical: he had been speaking against any Christian who stood by and let atrocities happen. He also realised pacifism was flawed because it tried to bring about peace in this world, not a divine peace that was part of the Kingdom of God. Christians need to be prophets, who speak into society when misuse of power is going on, and Bonhoeffer chose to be at the centre of that, not outside it.

This does not mean that Bonhoeffer thought that Christians must always ignore the rule of the State, but that in extreme circumstances, doing nothing is not acceptable. The State will never be able to reflect God's wishes fully as it is run by fallen human beings. The question a Christian must ask is whether it is God's will currently to obey the State. Indeed, all ethics must be about discovering the will of God.

● It is only in the moment of action that one can work out the will of God.
● Christians must give in to what they think is right to try to understand God's will.
● The Gospels show that the proper Christian response to Jesus is action, not beliefs.
● Christian discipleship is about deciding which leader you are going to follow.
● Following God's leadership above that of the State is therefore a radical approach to ethics.

Civil disobedience

Bonhoeffer clearly sees duty to God as coming above duty to the State. Standing by and doing nothing is not an option, even if civil disobedience has to be chosen. It was for this reason that Bonhoeffer joined the Resistance, spoke against Hitler in public and joined the plot to assassinate Hitler.

Bonhoeffer felt that this could be justified because a Christian's duty is not because of the State but it is towards the State. Jesus, too, seemed to ignore the possible consequences in his relationship with the State.

Revision activity

Summarise the learning in Sections 6.2, 6.3 and 6.4 in mind map form as you go along so you can see the links between them.

Key quote

We have literally no time to sit down and ask ourselves whether so-and-so is our neighbour or not. We must get into action and obey.

Bonhoeffer, *The Cost of Discipleship*

Key quote

Submit yourselves for the Lord's sake to every human authority: whether to the emperor as the supreme authority, or to governors, who are sent by him to punish those who do wrong and to commend those who do right.

1 *Peter* 2:13–14

Now test yourself

2 According to Bonhoeffer, when do Christians work out the will of God?
3 Why did Bonhoeffer join the Resistance movement?

TESTED

Now test yourself answers at **www.hoddereducation.co.uk/myrevisionnotes**

6.3 Church as community and source of spiritual discipline

The role of a Christian community is to give its members what they need to live good lives. Bonhoeffer thought that the Church needed to understand that the world is religionless and work within that context. **Religionless Christianity** is understood as:

- being in a world that has moved beyond the superstitions that religion brings with it and is moving towards rationalism
- needing to react to what society has replaced these superstitions with, such as Nazi ideologies
- having to lift itself beyond both its own past and current challenges
- needing to get rid of 'rusty swords' – Bonhoeffer's idea that ethics needs to be reinterpreted and move forward.

> **Key word**
>
> **Religionless Christianity**
> Bonhoeffer's idea that Christianity should get rid of old-fashioned ideas and separate itself from present ideologies

Bonhoeffer's role in the Confessing Church

The Confessing Church met together in 1934 at Barmen, to produce the Barmen Declaration, written by Karl Barth. In particular, the Confessing Church rejected the move by the German hierarchy to ban anyone not of Aryan descent from leadership within the Church. The core beliefs found in the Barmen Declaration include:

- Jesus is the only true leader and the only way to God.
- Christians must not follow any teaching that does not come from the revelation of Jesus.
- Other ideologies do not have authority over a person's life.

While the Barmen Declaration very firmly expressed its core beliefs, Bonhoeffer felt that it was not explicit enough in its idea of Church being for all people, not just the people of a nation. Its focus on beliefs, rather than action, was a weakness for Bonhoeffer, who by the end of his life thought that it had not done enough to promote disobedience to the State in a religionless world. He was perhaps particularly stung by the fact that the Confessing Church did not take a strong stand against the directive that all Church leaders should take the oath of obedience to Hitler.

> **Typical mistake**
>
> Weaker essays on Bonhoeffer tend to be more historical than theological. You need to be prepared to discuss key issues, such as whether Christianity comes out of the community, whether it is more about belief than action and so on.

Bonheoffer's religious community at Finkenwalde

In 1935 Bonhoeffer, on returning from America, was asked to look after a seminary (a place where Church leaders are trained) which soon moved to Finkenwalde. The seminary was illegal and secret because the State seminaries were only allowing Aryan people to train in their institutions. The seminary was closed in 1937 by the Gestapo because it went against the State.

The seminary allowed Bonhoeffer to reflect on what it meant to be a Christian community: for him, this was where spiritual discipline comes from. Spiritual discipline was, for Bonhoeffer:

- **prayer-centred**, including meditation
- **bible-based**, with lots of Bible study and discussion about Scripture
- **simple**, that is, there is no need to clutter a mind if you want to progress spiritually
- **focused on the whole-person**, that is, the body as well as the soul
- **communal**, based on the idea of mutual support and searching for the guidance of the Holy Spirit
- **action-based**, that is, the Church must look out towards the world and speak into the world.

Now test yourself

TESTED

4 What effect on Christianity had the move away from religion had, according to Bonhoeffer?
5 Out of what does spiritual discipline come?

6.4 The cost of discipleship

REVISED

Grace

Bonhoeffer rejects any understanding of grace as being easy to obtain. He calls this cheap grace. It is wrong to focus on the idea that grace is freely given and won in advance by Jesus because it suggests that whatever you do in life you will benefit fully from it. For Bonhoeffer, grace should be obtained by the Christian engaging with the suffering of Jesus because without doing this, the Christian is rejecting Jesus in some way. The grace that Bonhoeffer advocates is **costly grace**.

- The Christian must accept fully the leadership of Jesus, including his teachings.
- If Christians truly believed Jesus' words they would do anything to achieve the Kingdom of God.
- Costly grace means obeying God totally.

Sacrifice and suffering

Suffering was central to Jesus' life and it is through Jesus' suffering that Christians can fully understand God's revelation in him and obtain grace. Of course, for Bonhoeffer, this was expressed in his experiences against Nazism, in his imprisonment and eventual execution.

Bonhoeffer did not necessarily mean that a Christian's sufferings should be as extreme as Jesus' or even his own. However, his point was that a life of sacrifice is distinctive – the Christian must be different to the world around him or her. On the flip side, the Christian who has fully 'bought in' to costly grace will be willing to sacrifice much.

Bonhoeffer's work at Finkenwalde also emphasises that true spiritual discipline is a sacrifice in itself. Spiritual discipline will help the Christian to overcome the temptations of this world and to suffer in the same spirit of acceptance in which Jesus did.

Key quote

Cheap grace is the preaching of forgiveness without requiring repentance, baptism without Church discipline, Communion without confession.

Dietrich Bonhoeffer, *The Cost of Discipleship*

Key word

Costly grace The idea that the free gift of grace demands a response of true, sacrificial discipleship – total abandonment to Christ and to be Christ-like in your attitude

Solidarity

Solidarity is the word used to express Bonhoeffer's view that the Church must be 'for others'. His understanding of solidarity is shown in the way that he chose to return to Germany to be alongside other people and to work with them. Solidarity must be expressed to all people – the oppressed, those of other nations and beliefs, as well as each other.

Christians should do this by speaking out and questioning injustice when they perceive it, by finding the will of God and then following through with action. Bonhoeffer's view that Christians must be prophets who speak out is complemented by his view that Christians must take direct action. It was Bonhoeffer's solidarity with the Jews that led to his arrest.

For Bonhoeffer, solidarity is understood through the revelation of God in Jesus Christ. Understanding Jesus' interaction with political authorities, injustice in his time – as well as Jesus' example of taking action first, often before he discussed the issues – shows how Jesus was 'for others' (see Chapter 4, The person of Jesus Christ).

> **Key word**
>
> **Solidarity** The idea that Christians must be 'for others'

Now test yourself   TESTED ☐

6 For Bonhoeffer, what is the link between grace and suffering?
7 How does Bonhoeffer think we should engage with injustice?

6.5 Assessing Bonhoeffer: God's will and suffering

REVISED ☐

Can we always know God's will?

How can fallen human beings know God's will? Bonhoeffer, like Barth, believed that all we can know of God comes through God's deliberate decision to reveal himself. In the moment of action, Bonhoeffer felt that we should act in accordance with God's will so the Christian who practises spiritual discipline is likely to be able to identify God's revelation more clearly through discussion and prayer.

It could be said that to follow Bonhoeffer's approach implies that Bonhoeffer himself reveals God's will, although his interpretation of action might differ from somebody else's. It could also lead to Christians over-reacting to situations where calm negotiation might have more impact than direct action. Bonhoeffer's views could be said to be coloured by his extreme context (the Nazi regime).

However, community living might be the antidote to this potential danger. In a community, it is possible to discern together and mistakes are less likely to happen. Yet, nevertheless, in determining God's will, we seem to be suggesting more use of reason than revealed theology might like. Reason, as we saw with Barth in Chapter 3, is what led to the Nazi ideology.

One thing that Bonhoeffer clearly advocated was the role of the Christian as the prophet. A prophet's job is to speak the word of God and the prophets of the Old Testament did so with real confidence. Bonhoeffer's emphasis on simplicity and on Jesus might be said to show that with this discipline a Christian can indeed be confident that they can discern the will of God.

Does Bonhoeffer place too much emphasis on suffering?

Yes	No
Bonhoeffer lived in extreme circumstances and so, while it was appropriate to talk of suffering alongside Jesus in some way in the context of fighting the Nazis and possibly dying, this is not relevant outside the situation.	Suffering is a part of life for anyone who experiences injustice and for everyone at some level at some point in their lives.
Most Christians need to live their lives in 'everyday' circumstances and suffering should not be part of this approach.	For Bonhoeffer, suffering goes alongside solidarity and so the emphasis is on the whole picture of his thought, not just suffering.
It is unhealthy to 'seek out' situations that might lead to suffering.	Jesus told people to take up their own crosses and follow him, so Jesus himself encouraged his followers to embrace their suffering.
Bonhoeffer's emphasis on the suffering (and death) of Jesus might leave no room to understand the resurrection as a place where suffering is no more.	Bonhoeffer's thought is more than just about suffering – he is interested in the Christian engaging with Jesus Christ on all levels because Jesus is the total revelation of God.
The New Testament is full of references to God's grace being freely given, suggesting that the idea of costly grace requiring something from humans is not appropriate.	If you take your eye off the idea of suffering you could end up being the person who does not act – which is the starting point for Bonhoeffer's thought.

Revision activity

Practise this material by putting the section on knowing God's will into table form and the section on suffering into paragraph form to show you can manipulate the arguments on paper.

Now test yourself

TESTED

8 Why might Bonhoeffer's views about spiritual discipline help in deciding the will of God?

6.6 Assessing Bonhoeffer: his relevance for today

REVISED

Civil disobedience

Jesus and Paul both thought that Christians must exist within society. Paul said that if someone rebels against the State they are rebelling against God (see *Romans* 13:1–2). Jesus said that we give to Caesar (the State) what belongs to Caesar and to God what belongs to God (see *Matthew* 22:21). Both these passages seem to suggest that Christians should not act against the State and yet Jesus does that himself when he comes into conflict with the authorities around him. Jesus identified situations that he needed to be a prophet within, such as in the interpretation of the law or the treatment of outcasts, and Bonhoeffer certainly did the same in his very different context.

Other arguments could include:

- Jesus approached things from within the State; Bonhoeffer separated himself from the State. Perhaps Jesus's example is the one Christians should follow.
- Civil disobedience lowers the Christian to the level of terrorist.
- Bonhoeffer was working in an extreme situation.
- Christians should never begin with the assumption that they will disobey.

However, if Christians truly are going to build the Kingdom of God on earth, they will need to do so with some assertiveness. Whether or not Bonhoeffer's views of religionless society are accepted, Christians certainly believe in a truth that must be communicated to others and that truth includes a way of life that counters injustice.

Other arguments in favour of civil disobedience might be:

- Action is the only way that essential Christian truths can be heard.
- It accepts God as the ultimate authority, even though democracy is important.
- If costly grace is accepted as an approach, Christians do need to act.

Bonhoeffer in the twenty-first century

- Bonhoeffer's call to reject cheap grace and to embrace spiritual discipline could be valuable to people in today's society who could be said to live superficial and materialistic lives.
- For Christians, the idea of refocusing obedience onto the person of Jesus Christ and the will of God could be attractive.
- Community life and solidarity could be attractive as people seem to become more isolated.
- Inequality in the world is a reality that needs to be addressed.
- National boundaries and cultural boundaries are very different today; the Church should place itself beyond these.
- Church attendance and Christian faith is declining in some areas; perhaps Christianity does need to move away from its past.

For Christians seeking to use the teachings of Bonhoeffer, it is important to consider the extent to which he was writing within an extreme time. If he was, can any of his message appropriately transfer to a modern context? Should Christian ethics use the vocabulary of war and violence as much as Bonhoeffer could be said to have done?

Alternatively, it could be argued that Bonhoeffer's context forced a radical rethink of Christianity that is still relevant, even though the specific situation has passed.

> **Key quote**
>
> Since God, however, as ultimate reality is no other than the self-announcing, self-witnessing, self-revealing God in Jesus Christ, the question of good can only find its answer in Christ.
>
> Bonhoeffer, *Ethics*

> **Exam tip**
>
> Try to personalise the list of bullet points by including examples that you can draw on to illustrate the points. For example, the rejection of materialism could be illustrated by a comment on the twenty-first century obsession with possessions.

Now test yourself

TESTED

9 Where do Christians, according to Bonhoeffer, have to turn to get the answers they need?

6.7 Summary and exam tips

Exam checklist

- Compare Bonhoeffer's approach to duty to God and duty to the State.
- Explain Bonhoeffer's thinking about leadership, obedience and God's will.
- Evaluate whether civil obedience is right for Christians.
- Explain Bonhoeffer's understanding of spiritual discipline.
- Analyse the importance of Bonhoeffer's time at Finkenwalde.
- Explain Bonhoeffer's views on the cost of discipleship.
- Evaluate 'costly grace' and suffering in Bonhoeffer's thought.
- Critically explore Bonhoeffer's emphasis on solidarity.

Sample work

Students often struggle to know quite what to say in an essay conclusion. On the one hand, many conclusions say very little and are more of a summary. Equally, on the other hand, it is unreasonable for an A-level student to have taken a complete view on every single topic they have studied, especially in the context of a timed essay. You will see below that the improved conclusion is still not very long – it is better to fit in an extra main paragraph than to spend valuable time concluding.

First attempt	Improvement
In conclusion, Bonhoeffer was writing in Nazi times and resisted Hitler's ideology, which is why he practised civil disobedience.	Ultimately, Bonhoeffer's civil disobedience was relevant to his time under the Nazis, but it is clear that his civil disobedience was not one that can be carried over to modern times.

Going further: Barmen Declaration

Look at these extracts from the Barmen Declaration (1934) and read them in the context both of the work in this chapter and of the work you did on Karl Barth in Chapter 3 (remember, Barth wrote much of this).

'In fidelity to their Confession of Faith, members of Lutheran, Reformed, and United Churches sought a common message for the need and temptation of the Church in our day.'	'Scripture tells us that, in the as yet unredeemed world in which the Church also exists, the State has by divine appointment the task of providing for justice and peace.'
'Be not deceived by loose talk, as if we meant to oppose the unity of the German nation! If you find that we are speaking contrary to Scripture, then do not listen to us!'	'We reject the false doctrine, as though there were areas of our life in which we would not belong to Jesus Christ, but to other lords – areas in which we would not need justification and sanctification through him.'
'We may not keep silent, since we believe that we have been given a common message to utter in a time of common need and temptation.'	'We reject the false doctrine, as though the Church were permitted to abandon the form of its message and order to its own pleasure or to changes in prevailing ideological and political convictions.'
'Jesus Christ, as he is attested for us in Holy Scripture, is the one Word of God which we have to hear and which we have to trust and obey in life and in death.'	'We reject the false doctrine, as though the Church could and would have to acknowledge as a source of its proclamation, apart from and besides this one Word of God, still other events and powers, figures and truths, as God's revelation.'
'The Church's commission, upon which its freedom is founded, consists in delivering the message of the free grace of God to all people in Christ's stead.'	

Now test yourself answers at **www.hoddereducation.co.uk/myrevisionnotes**

7 Religious pluralism

7.1 Introduction

This chapter begins with a consideration of the **theology of religion**, before considering how this might play out in society.

Christianity preaches the uniqueness of the **Christ-event**, but beneath this comes the fundamental question of, in a world where we are more aware of other religions, whether Christianity or one denomination of Christianity has a particular claim to have 'got it right'.

Underpinning this chapter come two pairs of questions:
- Does one religion or tradition have a greater claim to the truth? Does one lead to salvation better than or in place of the others?
- What is necessary for salvation and what is sufficient (good enough)? Is a particular belief necessary? Is any quest for the truth sufficient? Was Jesus' death and resurrection necessary – and do you have to believe in it to go to heaven?

> **Key word**
>
> **Theology of religion** The branch of theology that examines the status of different religions in relation to each other

The specification says

Topic	Content	Key knowledge
Religious pluralism and theology	• The teaching of contemporary Christian theology of religion on:	
	– exclusivism	– The view that only Christianity fully offers the means of salvation
	– inclusivism	– The view that, although Christianity is the normative means of salvation, 'anonymous' Christians may also receive salvation
	– pluralism	– The view that there are many ways to salvation, of which Christianity is one path
	Learners should have the opportunity to discuss issues related to religious pluralism and Christian theology of religion, including: • whether or not, if Christ is the 'truth', there can be any other means of salvation • whether or not a loving God would ultimately deny any human being salvation • whether or not all good people will be saved • whether or not theological pluralism undermines central Christian beliefs.	
Religious pluralism and society	• The development of contemporary multi-faith societies	• The reasons for this development – for example, migration
	• Christian responses, including: – responses of Christian communities to inter-faith dialogue	• How Christian communities have responded to the challenge of encounters with other faiths, for example: – Catholic Church: *Redemptoris Missio*, 55–57 – Church of England: *Sharing the Gospel of Salvation*

Topic	Content	Key knowledge
	– the scriptural reasoning movement	– Its methods and aims – How the mutual study and interpretation of different religions' sacred literature can help understanding of different and conflicting religious truth claims

Learners should have the opportunity to discuss issues related to Christian responses to multi-faith societies and inter-faith dialogue, including:
- whether or not inter-faith dialogue has contributed practically towards social cohesion
- whether or not Christian communities should seek to convert people from other faiths
- whether or not scriptural reasoning relativises religious beliefs
- whether or not Christians should have a mission to those of no faith.

Revision activity

Take the information on the next three pages and put it into one mind map. Then make links between different aspects by drawing lines. Use one colour for similarities and one colour for differences. The differences could be used to analyse in detail in an essay.

7.2 Exclusivism

REVISED ☐

Christian exclusivism is the idea that only Christianity holds the truth and only Christianity can offer salvation. Calvinists teach that the Bible is clear that fallen humanity was restored through the unique sacrifice of Jesus, who also taught, 'I am the way and the truth and the life. No one comes to the Father except through me' (*John* 14:6). Due to the Fall, humans are sinful and therefore nobody deserves to be saved; this is how exclusivists justify the fact that some people have never had the opportunity to meet Jesus or have the Christian message explained to them. This is an example of **restricted access exclusivism**.

Some exclusivists believe that Jesus' salvation restored the whole of humanity, past, present and future. For these Christians, the emphasis shifts to God wishing to save everyone – **universal access exclusivism**. Perhaps people's non-religious lifestyles are appropriately moral and spiritual and they will have the Christian message explained to them at the moment of death, or after death: this gives everyone the opportunity to become a Christian.

Key words

Restricted access exclusivism Salvation comes from hearing the Christian message and accepting it into your life

Universal access exclusivism The idea that God wishes everyone to be saved

Catholic views on exclusivism

The Catholic Church teaches that there is no salvation outside of the Church – a person must be baptised and live a faithful Catholic life if they are to be in with a chance of going to heaven. This view excludes all other Christian denominations.

Since the 1960s, the Catholic Church has acknowledged that other denominations and religions hold aspects of the truth, but that the full expression of truth (and salvation) can only be found in the Catholic Church itself.

Key quote

The Catholic Church recognises in other religions that search, among shadows and images, for the God who is unknown yet near since he gives life and breath and all things and wants all men to be saved.

Catechism of the Catholic Church, 843

Assessing exclusivism

Some key weaknesses of exclusivism include:
- The fact that exclusivism leads to wars and conflict and treating others as less valuable people.
- The suggestion that if God condemns people who couldn't have heard the Christian message to hell then God is not loving.

- If God cannot be fully understood then it is impossible to say that anyone can have full control of the truth (and therefore salvation).
- The Bible suggests that people might be judged based on their actions (for example, the Sheep and the Goats) and not their beliefs.
- It does not seem fair that the Catholic Church should say that other religions are a preparation for the Gospel but that people cannot be saved if they are not part of the Church.

However, exclusivism clearly does make sense if Christianity is right. If Jesus is the Son of God then it makes sense that Christianity holds the truth in a way others don't. It could be argued that universal access exclusivism is also respectful of other faiths (because it allows for people to seek the truth, even if they are wrong), as is the Catholic approach (because it allows for some truth to be found in other religious practices).

1 Which denomination says that there is no salvation outside of the Church?

7.3 Inclusivism

REVISED

Inclusivism is the idea that, although Christianity is the one true faith and the **normative way to salvation**, it is possible for non-Christians who are **anonymous** or invisible Christians to be saved. Ultimately, all people have a spiritual aspect to themselves, which makes them search for the truth. If done in an appropriate way, even if from within another faith setting, non-Christians can access the same benefits of Jesus' death on the cross.

Karl Rahner

Rahner (1904–1984) was a German Catholic thinker.
- Christianity is the one true religion (because of Jesus) but even before Jesus, Christianity had a history and the Old Testament figures must have been able to be saved.
- Other religions can help people to salvation but only until a person encounters the Christian message, at which point they can accept or reject it.
- Christian missionaries must not assume that the non-Christians they encounter have no experience of the truth.
- The Church needs to be the visible expression of what other institutions have in an invisible way.

Rahner draws on *Acts* 17 where Paul, making a speech in Athens to pagan people, commends his listeners for an altar he found marked 'to an unknown God': they had been worshipping the Christian God without knowing it and his role now is to explain who this God is. Similarly, it is valid for those of other backgrounds to worship God in their own way until they encounter fully the Christian message.

If God truly wants people to be saved, Rahner believes that:
- institutions can be a form of anonymous Christianity – because they have structures that explore truth and salvation they, just like the Jewish faith pre-Christianity, can be a means of grace
- individuals can be anonymous Christians – because people who do not identify as members of a religious institution can be said to be good and moral and therefore on their own search for the truth.

Key words

Normative way to salvation
The usual or ideal way to be saved, but not necessarily the only one

Anonymous Christian
Someone who is open to God's grace but not a Christian

Key quote

Somehow all men must be capable of being members of the Church.

Rahner, *Theological Investigations*

Making links

Acts 17 is also examined in Chapter 3, Section 3.5.

Assessing inclusivism

Inclusivism balances the unique Christ-event and the idea that a loving God would want to save people. It acknowledges the idea of a *sensus divinitas* (see Chapter 3, Knowledge of God's existence). It also conforms to Biblical ideas that the Jewish people were chosen by God and presumably therefore saved without knowing Christ and passages like the Sheep and the Goats, which say that judgement is based on our actions, not beliefs.

However, inclusivism has been accused of being patronising to other faiths – why could a Christian not be an anonymous Hindu? Rahner potentially could also be accused of decentralising Christ from salvation and of undermining the role of the Church (founded by Jesus) in the world.

Arguably, inclusivism is a dressed-up version of universal access exclusivism because non-Christian religions remain inferior to Christian ones. It could be argued that Rahner is simply playing with words to try to make Christianity look less unapproachable.

Typical mistake

Be careful not to assume that exclusivism and inclusivism are completely non-overlapping. Universal access exclusivism and inclusivism have a lot in common!

Now test yourself

2 Who coined the term 'anonymous Christians'?
3 What phrase is used if an entire religion has a structure that leads people anonymously to God?

TESTED ☐

7.4 Pluralism

REVISED ☐

The most common image to explain pluralism is that of the blind men and the elephant. The idea is that if a group of blind men come across an elephant and each touch a different part of it then each will gain a different understanding of what the elephant is like, even though each is equally valid (and equally limited). Pluralism is the idea that there are many ways to salvation and Christianity is just one of these paths.

Hick

John Hick (1922–2012) is the best-known advocate of pluralism. He is said to have been inspired by his work in multi-cultural Birmingham.
● A natural theologian, Hick felt that all that needed to be known should be able to be deduced from this world.
● People believe because of religious experience, but religious experience is interpreted through individual faith traditions – religious experience is common to all faiths.
● Therefore, different people are experiencing and interpreting the same reality in different ways.
● Cultural differences provide the different lenses through which we experience the divine.

Hick was influenced by Kant, who distinguished between the noumena (what a thing actually is) and the phenomena (how we individually experience it). Therefore, the noumena of the divine (the Real or the Eternal One) is one thing, but it is experienced through different phenomena (religions). Pluralism understands each of these phenomenal ways as equally valid.

Christianity is generally Christocentric (centred on Christ) but Hick felt that the central point should not be Christ or Christianity but God – Hick argued for the theology of religion being theocentric (centred on God). Christianity's claims on truth, such as the incarnation, the nature of Jesus and resurrection, need to be reinterpreted as mythical – stories with truth elements – rather than factual ones. This means that Christianity is on the side, looking inwards towards God, like other religions. Hick's empirical evidence for this is quite simply that other religions produce equally good people as Christianity; why should Christianity be superior in any way?

Assessing pluralism

Hick's approach assumes that Kant's philosophical approach is correct. It also assumes that there is a 'Real' in terms of a divinity of some sort; this is rejected by many forms of Buddhism. Arguably, if Christianity (and other religions) are simply myths then any aspect of truth becomes lost and there is nothing to believe in, except a completely distant 'Real'.

Christians might challenge Hick on the basis that they argue that the Christ-event is unique in a way that other religions do not claim. It is faith, especially in the resurrection, that is the challenge for believers. Atheists might challenge him because it seems to be an assumption that there is any reality behind it all – why not simply reject religion outright?

However, Hick's approach is attractive. In a global society, it recognises that the foundations of many religious beliefs are outdated and narrow, and may need to be reconsidered.

> **Typical mistake**
>
> Be careful not to say that Hick argues that all religions are true. He doesn't! He says that all religions contain different aspects of the truth.

Now test yourself

TESTED

4 How does Hick account for cultural differences and their perception of God?
5 What did Hick say a theology of religion should be centred on instead of Christ?

7.5 Discussing theology of religion

REVISED

If Christ is the 'truth' can there be any other means of salvation?

Exclusivists might say:

- The claim that God became a human is too different from other truth claims of other faiths not to be taken seriously.
- Just because somebody disagrees with you, it does not mean that you should reach a compromise – this is the trend towards relativism in modern society.
- Such a serious question as to whether or not someone spends eternity in heaven or hell requires definite answers.
- Pluralism sounds nice, but moves away from any possibility of there being truth.
- Pluralism tries to approach evidence from a natural theology standpoint but fails to notice essential and revealed Christian truths, such as the effect of the Fall on the world and humanity.

However, an exclusivist approach requires revealed theology, which has its own issues (see Chapter 3, Knowledge of God's existence). People who answer 'Yes' to the question in the heading above might say:

- Inclusivism shows that Christ's truth is for all of humanity – Christ's incarnation took place out of love and this same love must look after those who are not Christians.

- Pluralism rejects the idea that Christ is 'the' truth – the words of the Bible might not be literally true, for example, including the words attributed to Jesus.
- If God truly does not save others then this God is not worthy of our worship.
- Hick's approach to the 'Real' is a useful way of understanding how different worldviews might work together appropriately.

Would a loving God ultimately deny any human being salvation?

In many approaches, there seems to be the assumption that salvation is determined by beliefs. However, there is equally as much to suggest that salvation is linked to our actions. In Christian ethics, it is often thought to be the case that the intention behind our actions is important. Why should this not be the case with belief? If our intention is to seek the truth, surely God, who knows everything, will reward this?

Pluralists feel that it is possible that God is present in different ways and in different cultures, so that people can understand salvation in an appropriate way. It might not be useful for someone with a non-western worldview to think of reward, punishment, time and judgement in a western sense.

Some Christians believe that Original Sin made too great an impact on the world – see Chapter 1 for more discussion on this and Chapter 2 for more about who goes to heaven or hell.

One of the biggest problems for Christians is the problem of evil and the problem of innocent suffering. For any Christian to say that some go to hell because they weren't Christians – and they couldn't have been Christians – is perhaps to develop the problem of innocent suffering.

> **Making links**
>
> The problem of evil and nature of God are discussed in full in the Philosophy of Religion book, Chapter 6.

> **Exam tip**
>
> This section shows the importance of being able to draw on learning from across the course to help to answer questions.

Now test yourself

TESTED

6 Why might an exclusivist reject relativism?

7.6 Inter-faith dialogue

REVISED

The development of contemporary multi-faith societies

A global perspective is probably something we – that is, those who are used to the internet, American (especially) cultural influences and being able to pick from many types of cuisine – take for granted. This globalisation spread in the second half of the twentieth century far faster than before (despite the ease of the British Empire) because of technological developments. With this globalisation comes the ability both to encounter people of other faiths and also to find out information about other faiths.

In addition to this, as people have moved away from the tendency to live in their local area for their whole life, there has been more mixing of people with already-established communities, such as Indian or Jewish communities which have been around for some time, but have been concentrated in particular areas of the country.

> **Exam tip**
>
> Background information is useful when it contributes to your argument, but make sure you do not turn an essay on inter-faith dialogue into one on why Britain is multi-cultural!

Modern abilities to communicate and travel more easily and more cheaply mean that more and more people have encountered other cultures and, with them, other faiths, and this has generally led to more tolerance in society, such that people of other faiths feel able to move to a traditionally Protestant Christian country. The trend to this tolerance arguably started with the Enlightenment, but has been facilitated by modern lifestyle.

Migration

Underneath all of this is the issue of migration. People have migrated to the UK for many reasons: for safety (in the case of refugees), for economic development (because the standard of living is higher in the UK) or simply because other members of their family have already lived here for a while. As such, communities of those from other cultures have increased and multi-faith society has become natural to much of the UK. It is important to recognise that migration has also led to Christianity seeing new influences and new denominations, as much as a significant increase in members of other faith traditions.

Living in a multi-faith society challenged John Hick to become a pluralist and potentially will challenge British Christians as these societies become more embedded.

Inter-faith dialogue

Inter-faith dialogue, the conversation between different faiths, has taken a new direction, perhaps because of three reasons.

1 Migration has exposed more people in the West to ways of thinking from the Far East that are entirely different from their normal use of language.
2 The Holocaust forced Christianity to think about its relationship with Judaism because strands of institutional anti-Semitism seemed still to survive (whereby Jews are seen as those who have somehow 'failed' to become Christians).
3 Modern tensions with Islam, still being played out, show the importance of seeking common ground and common teachings of loving your neighbour and placing God at the centre of life.

The approach taken to inter-faith dialogue will depend on the theology of religion:

Theology of religion	Aims and purposes of inter-faith dialogue
Exclusivism	To open the conversation so that people from other faiths can be converted. To begin to understand where those from other faiths are coming from so that they can find common ground and show how that common ground points towards the Christian message.
Inclusivism	To create dialogue between both institutions (anonymous Christianity) and individuals (anonymous Christians) to understand where each comes from and how to communicate the Christian message relevantly. The dialogue can provide openings for ways to work together, perhaps charitably, in a context of mutual respect.
Pluralism	To discover different understandings of the truth and so to enhance your own understanding of the 'Real'. Inter-faith dialogue could potentially serve to stop conflicts between different religions and lead to peace. Some might approach this from looking at shared ways of life before tackling points of theology.

Catholic Church: *Redemptoris missio*

This Papal encyclical (authoritative letters from the Pope to his Church) from 1990, written by Pope John Paul II, focused on the missionary work of the Church in a multi-faith world. Catholics must remember they have a mission to non-Catholics, remain open and honest and respectful, but never shy away from the truth of the Gospel. The section set for study on the specification is entitled 'Dialogue with our brothers and sisters of other religions'. Some key points are:

- There is no conflict between belief in Christ and inter-faith dialogue.
- Inter-faith dialogue is an opportunity to give a full account of Christian belief.
- All religions hold aspects of the truth and are led by the Holy Spirit, so dialogue needs to be respectful (and not have an ulterior motive of converting people).
- Dialogue helps the Church to find out which aspects of the truth are held by other individuals and institutions.
- A key aim is to build a happy society.
- Mission is for all members of the Church, not just priests.
- Missionaries need to be persistent in their work.

Church of England: *Sharing the Gospel of Salvation*

This document from 2010 acknowledges that modern Britain is a multi-faith society which everyone shares. The document affirms that salvation has been achieved through the Christ-event and therefore Christians must proclaim this. The role of the Christian in it is to:

- be sensitive to those around them – do not try to 'make a sale'
- develop good relationships with people in the spirit of welcoming in the hope that they will be baptised in the future – to 'go beyond tolerance'
- live a good Christian lifestyle as distinct and authentic Christians
- work for the common good of society
- remember that they could be a missionary in a number of different contexts, not just the more obvious ones and to do this through being proud of your tradition.

There are four aspects to dialogue:

1 Daily life, where you meet people in your life and talk about beliefs
2 Common good, where you work with those of other faiths to benefit the community
3 Mutual understanding, where you get together for formal discussions (for example, scriptural reasoning)
4 Spiritual life, where you pray and worship together

> **Revision activity**
>
> Develop the table above to explore what the scholars in Chapter 4, Sections 4.2, 4.3 and 4.4 would say about inter-faith dialogue.

> **Key quote**
>
> Dialogue is a path toward the kingdom and will certainly bear fruit, even if the times and seasons are known only to the Father.
>
> *Redemptoris Missio*, 57

> **Key quote**
>
> It makes example – the example of the Church as a whole, as well as of individual Christians – the shared vocabulary through which the Christian story may be known.
>
> *Sharing the Gospel of Salvation*, 13

> **Now test yourself**
>
> 7 Why did migration make Hick into a pluralist?
> 8 Which denomination warns Christians not to try to make a sale when witnessing to the Gospel?
>
> TESTED

7.7 The scriptural reasoning movement

REVISED

Scriptural reasoning began in the United States and has been adapted by the Cambridge Inter-faith Programme. It is a tool to help with inter-faith dialogue and will suit some, but not all people. Its purpose is not to convert anyone but to help those from different faith backgrounds to understand where and why they disagree about different truth claims and to discuss them in a safe place. The movement started with Jews, Christians and Muslims because of their shared history, but has also successfully worked with people from other faith backgrounds.

Methods

A session will focus on one text from each tradition and will look at the text in the common language of the participants, with the original language close to hand. A facilitator will lead and people will read the texts and discuss their messages. As the discussion progresses, some of the context of the passages will be explored to try to understand where the text is coming from. Texts are understood in two ways:

- as texts themselves – looking at the language, the themes, the historical context, structure and so on
- as being read – looking at how the text is read and understood in the modern life of the faith.

If the participants are academics, texts will be approached in one way; if they are not scholars, it will be different. One of the important 'rules' of a session is that the focus must remain on the texts and it should not become a general discussion of the religion. Participants are encouraged not to speak 'for' their faith by saying 'Christians believe X', but to say 'As a Christian, this text says X'.

Aims

The aims of scriptural reasoning are very much to maintain a spirit of dialogue. There is no attempt to convert people to one way of thinking and there is no intention to produce official documents on behalf of a religion or group of religions. Three core aims of scriptural reasoning might be identified:

1 Wisdom (everyone is united in their desire for wisdom coming out of discussion)
2 Collegiality (everyone is an equal participant; all contributions are equal)
3 Hospitality (it is non-judgemental)

Assessing scriptural reasoning

Scriptural reasoning is difficult to criticise. It has very clear guidelines about what it aims to achieve, the safety of the dialogue and the limits of the discussions. It has clear spiritual benefits for individual participants and encourages tolerance. As many religions have texts at their heart, it encourages participants to engage deeply in the origins of these religions.

Some criticisms might be identified as:

- If it is impossible to be wrong, what is the point of the sessions and when does an interpretation begin to be inappropriate?
- Is there any point in having these discussions if there is no official teaching of the religion? In some situations, people might leave with an incorrect view of another faith.
- Scriptural reasoning will not work for people from certain traditions within faiths, such as exclusivists or literalists.
- It could relativise religious beliefs because the methods require that all points are treated as equally important.

Now test yourself

TESTED

9 Which three religions with a shared history does scriptural reasoning mostly bring together?
10 True or false: Scriptural reasoning is designed to create debates about the truth of different religions.

Has inter-faith dialogue contributed practically towards social cohesion?

Christians aim to live life to promote the common good and therefore to live as part of society. This is a fundamental aim of Roman Catholic ethics and an underpinning element of *Sharing the Gospel of Salvation* for the Church of England. Therefore, it would be hoped that any engagement in inter-faith relations would contribute positively towards **social cohesion**. However, modern secular society has less space in it for religion and religious practices are less influential in day-to-day life.

Some might suggest that anything that promotes tolerance in contemporary society is important. There is suspicion of some faith communities simply because they are different and overcoming ignorance is important. Any shared charitable work for the local community will promote social cohesion. Those living in a local community with a range of faith communities will probably be able to point towards more examples of inter-faith work promoting the local community than others.

Some might argue that the aim of inter-faith dialogue is not to promote social cohesion, but to work on an even smaller scale – a few individuals together – and that this is beneficial. Others might suggest that it is about exploring differences safely and is not about overcoming them, as social cohesion might suggest.

Should Christians try to convert people?

For most Christians, **evangelism** is a central aim. Jesus sent his disciples out to spread the message both during his ministry and in his final words before leaving them (known as The Great Commission). The Roman Catholic Church speaks of the 'right' of all to hear the Gospel message and the Church of England agrees that the Christ-event needs to be communicated with others.

Converting people of other religions assumes that Christianity is the one way to the truth. Exclusivists would argue that it is important to offer the chance of salvation to all. Inclusivists would emphasise the need for sensitivity and would not wish social cohesion to be upset, but would still aim for all to hear the true message. Pluralists would not agree with the conversion of other faiths to Christianity because other faiths are also valid ways to express truth. As society encourages religious belief to be more private, Christians often evangelise by example – living lives that make others ask, 'Why are they like that?' and opening the opportunity for dialogue. The Christian mission to those of no faith is more urgent for some Christians because they might argue that many atheists and agnostics do not have access to the Truth even in its dimmest form. Many church communities welcome people into their buildings just to break down barriers and perceptions about what it is to be a Christian and many discovery courses about faith appeal to those with no tradition of religious belief.

Key word

Social cohesion A society that works well together – has a sense of identity and community

Key word

Evangelism Spreading the Christian message

Key quote

Therefore go and make disciples of all nations, baptising them in the name of the Father and of the Son and of the Holy Spirit.

Matthew 28:19

Revision activity

In discussing inter-faith dialogue, try to make a mind map of the arguments and then in a different colour add in the information from sections 7.6 and 7.7.

7.9 Summary and exam tips

Exam checklist

- Explain each of exclusivism, inclusivism and pluralism.
- Compare different approaches to theology of religion.
- Evaluate whether there is salvation without belief in Christ.
- Analyse whether a loving God would deny any human being salvation.
- Explain inter-faith dialogue and multi-faith societies.
- Explain the aims and methods of scriptural reasoning.
- Analyse whether Christians should aim to convert people.
- Evaluate whether inter-faith dialogue has contributed to social cohesion.

Sample work

One of the biggest pitfalls when writing essays is ensuring that you answer the specific question set and not the one you had revised for! Here we imagine an essay asking you to analyse *Redemptoris Missio* 55–57.

> **Key quote**
>
> In the beginning was the Word ... and the Word was God ... The Word became flesh and made his dwelling among us. We have seen his glory ...
>
> *John 1:1, 14*

First attempt	Improvement
The idea that *Redemptoris Missio* makes inter-faith dialogue impossible might be said to be true because it keeps Jesus' death as a compulsory point of belief, which might make it seem inaccessible. *Sharing the Gospel of Salvation* also does this when it says that the focus must be on the Christian story. This means that inter-faith dialogue will be too difficult to maintain well as people will not think Christians are approachable.	The idea that *Redemptoris Missio* makes inter-faith dialogue impossible might be said to be true because it keeps Jesus' death as a compulsory point of belief, which might make it seem inaccessible. It celebrates the role of the Christian missionary because the Christian message still needs to be communicated in full. This means that inter-faith dialogue will be too difficult for Catholics to maintain well as people will not think Christians are approachable and open to other viewpoints.

Going further: Barth

Barth is an example of where the boundaries between exclusivism and inclusivism can blur.

- Barth's starting point is a Calvinist approach to exclusivism and election.
- God is only knowable through his choice to reveal himself to people when he wishes. Humans cannot choose when to identify God.
- The Trinity and the person of Jesus are unique to Christianity and this makes the Christian understanding of God's self-revelation unique.
- Jesus as the Word made Flesh is revealed through the incarnation, the Bible and the Church, but the only completely accurate way of understanding God's self-revelation is through the Bible.
- Jesus was entirely unique and God can only be properly known through Jesus Christ.
- The Christian revelation overcomes all other faiths.

However, Barth does not seem to have thought that only Christians can access God's grace: the Holy Spirit can work anywhere and God can choose to reveal himself wherever he wants, not just through Christian methods. For this reason, Barth begins to come across as an inclusivist: election, for Barth, is something open to anyone who is willing to receive God's grace.

> **Making links**
>
> For more on Barth, see Chapter 3, Knowledge of God's existence.

> **Exam tip**
>
> Equally, Barth could be argued to tend towards universalism and the idea that all will be saved, which makes the idea of exclusivism difficult to maintain.

8 Gender

8.1 Introduction

REVISED

Christianity has had a turbulent history when it comes to its treatment of women. Arguably, the earliest Christians were more inclusive of women than some Christian denominations now. This has led to controversial discussion about family life, motherhood, and the roles of women in society and in families that do not have a mother and father as the adults.

Some Christians do all they can to maintain the view of gender and family that is portrayed in the Bible. They might do this because they come from Christian backgrounds that view the Bible as authoritative for modern life; alternatively, they might refer to the order of creation and other evidence that this is the 'natural' way to be.

However, other Christians would view this as a root of many of the problems in the Church – Jesus did not approve of oppression, but this approach oppresses different groups of people.

It can be argued that Christianity should adapt to society so that it can speak to young people and future generations; however, if God has established a true order of society, perhaps Christians should not bow to moral relativism. The fast-paced change to society, especially in the West, is challenging Christianity to examine its identity and its mission.

> **Revision activity**
>
> Make a table for and against the idea that Christianity should change with the times in terms of gender and family life.

The specification says

Topic	Content	Key knowledge
Gender and society	● The effects of changing views of gender and gender roles on Christian thought and practice, including:	
	– Christian teaching on the roles of men and women in the family and society	● including reference to: – *Ephesians* 5:22–33 – *Mulieris Dignitatem* 18–19
	– Christian responses to contemporary secular views about the roles of men and women in the family and society	● The ways in which Christians have adapted and challenged changing attitudes to family and gender, including issues of: – motherhood/parenthood – different types of family
	Learners should have the opportunity to discuss issues related to Christian responses to changing views of gender and gender roles, including: ● whether or not official Christian teaching should resist current secular views of gender ● whether or not secular views of gender equality have undermined Christian gender roles ● whether or not motherhood is liberating or restricting ● whether or not the idea of family is entirely culturally determined.	

Topic	Content	Key knowledge
Gender and theology	• The reinterpretation of God by feminist theologians, including: – the teaching of Rosemary Radford Ruether and Mary Daly on gender and its implications for the Christian idea of God	• Ruether's discussion of the maleness of Christ and its implications for salvation, including: – Jesus' challenge to the male warrior–messiah expectation – God as the female wisdom principle – Jesus as the incarnation of wisdom • Daly's claim that 'if God is male then male is God' and its implications for Christianity, including: – Christianity's 'Unholy Trinity' of rape, genocide and war – spirituality experienced through nature
	Learners should have the opportunity to discuss issues related to God, gender and feminist theology, including: • a comparison of Ruether's and Daly's feminist theologies – sexism and patriarchy in Christianity, as it has developed in the mainstream Churches – whether Christianity can be changed or should be abandoned • whether or not Christianity is essentially sexist • whether or not a male saviour can save women • whether or not only women can develop a genuine spirituality • whether or not the Christian God can be presented in female terms.	

8.2 Gender and gender roles

REVISED

The early feminist philosopher Mary Wollstonecraft published her work *A Vindication of the Rights of Women* in 1792 in which she argued that women fundamentally have the same rights as men. Educating women was the highest priority – as well as refocusing them away from obsession with looks and outward accomplishments. Wollstonecraft was an early challenge to the **patriarchy** of her day.

It was not until 1928 that women were fully able to vote as equals to men in the UK and the contraceptive pill was only made fully accessible in 1974. Women could take control of pregnancies from 1967 when abortion was made legal and in 1970 women were allowed to be paid equally to men.

Feminism is often divided into three historical waves.
1 First-wave feminism. Beginning in the second half of the twentieth century, this focused on equal rights for women, such as in the right to vote.
2 Second-wave feminism. During the 1960s, this challenged patriarchy and pressed for women to have rights over their own selves, not just to exist as homemakers; the result was developments in sexual health.
3 Third-wave feminism. This began in the 1990s and explores gender roles and identities; women need to change the approach they take to themselves, making sure they don't conform to the stereotype of 'white heterosexual woman from the West'.

There are different approaches to the relationship between men and women:
• *Men are superior to women.* A view dating back to the ancients, such as Plato and Aristotle, but also held by Aquinas, who described women as 'defective'.

> **Key word**
>
> **Patriarchy** Male-dominated; a patriarchal society is one where men have more power than women

> **Exam tip**
>
> While the background information is important, remember that you will be using it as part of an argument, not writing out a history of feminism.

- *Men and women are of equal value.* This is the idea that men and women are different, but of equal value, leading to mainly-male and mainly-female roles in the workplace and even in Church leadership.
- *Women are superior to men.* As advocated by Mary Daly (1928–2010); patriarchy in the Church has hidden women's superior knowledge.
- *Gender is not as straightforward as traditionally thought.* We can express ourselves as one or other gender, or as a mixture; it is artificial and misleading to assign characteristics to genders and not necessary to identify with the biological identity you have.

Christianity has sometimes been seen to struggle with where it should stand in relation to the above bullet points. Some Christians have accepted women in leadership roles in the Church; others believe it is a matter of theology, not equality, and that different rules apply in the context of the Church. Some Christians are accused of still supporting a patriarchal society. Contemporary Christians seem to be unsure how to respond to new issues such as gender identity and expression, sexuality and so on. As we are in the middle of the third-wave, Christians are often accused of being slow to respond (because they spend time discerning the will of God) and so Churches can frustrate those anxious to bring about change.

Now test yourself

TESTED

1 Which wave of feminism focused on women's rights over themselves?
2 What did Aquinas believe about men and women?

8.3 Christian teaching on the roles of men and women in the family and society

REVISED

Many Christians refer primarily to the story of creation in the Bible: man and woman were designed to work alongside each other in family life. However, many modern Christians will point to the understanding that the Bible should be read in the context of the time in which it was written and therefore can be forgiven for its narrow approach.

Ephesians 5:22–33

This passage, a set of instructions for Christian households, would have been a familiar approach to Paul's readers who were used to similar lists from Roman and Greek traditions. The passage is traditional in its outlook, although its interpretation over the years has varied.

- Wives should submit to their husbands.
- The husband is the head of his wife.

It also puts a Christian twist on the traditional views.

- The husband's leadership is like the leadership of Christ to the Church.
- Husbands should love their wives like Christ loved the Church.

This Christian twist is actually quite radical in outlook – Christ loved the Church so much he gave up his life for it, as a husband should do for his wife.

The familiar 'body of Christ' imagery also would have spoken to Paul's readers who were used to the idea that the Church is an inter-connected body of people; here it reminds us that marriage is a small section of a wider community and so family life is part of the wider life of Christianity.

Mulieris Dignitatem 18–19

This text is a Catholic 1988 letter of Pope John Paul II on the dignity and vocation of women in response to feminism (third-wave feminism would not have fully taken off by the time this was written). The emphasis was on respect for women – a respect that is mirrored by Mary, without whom the Christ-event would not have happened.

- Motherhood, a natural follow-on from marriage, which is part of the order of creation, comes from the total giving of a couple to each other, open to procreation, a way of sharing in God's act of creation.
- The psycho-physical structure of a woman is made for motherhood. Parenthood, although it is shared between the man and woman is more specially the woman's. The man should learn parenthood from the mother.
- The mother has precedence over the man as the first teacher of the child: this is the spiritual aspect of motherhood.
- It is Mary's acceptance of the message of the angel that begins the New Covenant (the new relationship between God and humans brought about by Jesus).
- This understanding of motherhood must continue for modern mothers and they must be appropriately supported when their immense maternal love is challenged.

> **Key quote**
>
> It is therefore necessary that the man be fully aware that in their shared parenthood he owes a special debt to the woman. No programme of 'equal rights' between women and men is valid unless it takes this fact fully into account.
>
> *Mulieris Dignitatem*, 18

> **Exam tip**
>
> You need to be able to identify these texts by their names as they appear in the specification and in the titles on this page.

Now test yourself

TESTED

3 Which key text says that men should love women like Christ loved the Church?
4 Which Pope observed that women are psycho-physically created by God for motherhood?

8.4 Motherhood/parenthood

REVISED

In *Mulieris Dignitatem*, the Catholic Church attempts to underline the special dignity, deliberately given by God at creation, to women to be mothers. This reflects many Christian approaches to the topic as the ability of women to be mothers is seen as a great privilege and not in any way making them lesser beings. However, in the context of suspicion of patriarchal institutions, some might feel that this approach is patronising, or limiting the abilities of women.

A response to this might be to reject any view of women that defines them as mothers first and foremost. Reading on in the document, one might feel that the stark alternative being suggested by the Pope for women is to be either mothers or virgins.

Fundamentalist Protestant traditions, which might read the *Ephesians* passage in a literal sense, would emphasise the role of the woman as wife and mother: her role is primarily to create a home suitable for the husband. Other Protestants might take a view similar to that of the Catholic Church, above.

A more liberal approach removes the idea of motherhood from the definition of women. In line with many moves within third-wave feminism, it understands gender roles in less black and white terms. Mary may have been a role model, but not for everyone; just like Peter wouldn't be a typical role model for all men.

> **Exam tip**
>
> There is a full range of views within Christianity; it is important to be able to show that some have been influenced by secular feminism and others have not.

Is motherhood liberating or restricting?

Liberating	Restricting
It is what women were created for and so it is a way of them fulfilling their purpose.	A woman must give up her own life, interests and personality to take care of her children.
It draws on the natural abilities of women to be caring and nurturing.	It slows down progress with careers; it affects bodily health.
Mulieris Dignitatem suggests that motherhood is extremely liberating for women.	When children leave home, a woman is left without a proper purpose.
Some argue that a woman's desire to be a mother is biological.	Others argue that the desire is purely the result of social conditioning.
A woman is able to provide the best start to the education of the next generation.	A woman's intelligence is wasted when at home with children.

The first three points on the 'restricting' side of the table come from the work of Simone de Beauvoir, whose work *The Second Sex* (1949) says that women over time have let themselves be made into the inferior gender, defined by their relationship with men as wife, lover and object. De Beauvoir argued that society forms people into their gender identities and she calls on modern women to redefine who they are and to be who they want to be – whether that is a mother or not.

The above table provides an overly simplistic view of motherhood, which is neither simple to describe nor the same for every woman. It also isolates motherhood – in many families, the mother has a partner to share the role with and this will help to define what it is to be a mother for that context.

Now test yourself

TESTED

5 Who thought that women had become sexual objects of men?

8.5 Different types of family

REVISED

Traditional Christians would emphasise the importance of the type of family they see in the Bible: heterosexual and married. They might accuse some feminists of changing the idea of love between a couple from selfless Christian love to a love based on the sexual aspect of the relationship. They argue that the Biblical model of marriage leads to support for struggling married couples in the community and a more stable society.

Other Christians accept that the traditional view of the family is not a reflection of the way people are made. If some are made homosexual and want to have children, then it follows that there will be loving families with same-gender parents. Any reluctance to endorse same-gender parents is a societal issue, rather than a faith one for these Christians; Jesus himself welcomed those who did not fully conform to society; love needs to remain at the centre.

Another argument might be that in the Bible there are many different types of family – men with more than one wife or with children from concubines, for example. The argument would go that the idea of family is not predominantly religious and is more cultural and Christianity must welcome any model that current society offers.

> **Revision activity**
>
> Try to break down this text-heavy section into something more diagrammatic, such as a mind map or chart. Add to it using your class notes and your own thoughts.

Roman Catholic teaching is that families should be heterosexual and married. The Church condemns those who live together outside marriage and does all that it can to prevent relationship breakdowns. Catholics do not believe that women should necessarily remain at home but think that motherhood as a 'career choice' needs to be celebrated as much as any other career choice.

Is the idea of family entirely culturally determined?

The family is seen as a microcosm of society – a society that is made up of families that work well is likely to work well itself. Recently, the notion of family has changed rapidly. Marriage has been permitted in the UK for homosexual couples only since 2014 (civil partnerships became legal in 2005) and this will lead to a greater number of children from same-gender parents and inevitably lead to a change in the way that we look at families. By this argument, the idea of family will be entirely determined by culture and Christians will need to decide how they react to what a family is.

However, Christians believe that most are called to parenthood and family life, to mirror God's love and creative work and so on. Many commandments in the Bible concern family life and Catholic natural law supports families. Holding love at the centre of family life also mirrors many Christians' approach to ethics. Those Christians who believe heterosexual marriage is a fundamental part of the order of creation will do all they can to defend this model of family life.

> **Typical mistake**
>
> It is important not to assume that the UK model of family is the only approach to family around in the twenty-first century – in some cultures, for example, a man is allowed more than one wife.

Now test yourself

TESTED

6 Which denomination says that motherhood is a valid and celebrated 'career choice'?

8.6 Reinterpretation of God by feminist theologians: Rosemary Radford Ruether

REVISED

A Catholic feminist theologian, Ruether wanted feminism to move Christianity away from the patriarchy that has grown over time: the focus for Christians should be God, not male leaders.

Jesus' challenge to the male warrior–messiah expectation

At Jesus' time, the Messiah was expected to be a liberator of the line of David who would save people from the Romans. Ruether says that this is not the Messiah, Jesus was. For Ruether:

- There was no expectation of the incarnation of God or of salvation through sacrifice.
- Jesus was not a military leader – he rejected use of force to win arguments.
- The Kingdom of God was a place of harmony, not power.
- Jesus rejected patriarchal God-talk by using 'Abba' for God – meaning 'daddy'; the dominant–subordinate dynamic was rejected in favour of a more familiar relationship.

Therefore, the military (and therefore male) view of God is not needed; the fact that Jesus was biologically a man does not matter.

God as the female wisdom principle

The person of 'wisdom' (*Sophia* in Greek) is very much present in later Old Testament books, perhaps left over from the earliest time of Judaism when monotheism wasn't fully established. Wisdom is always portrayed as female. For Ruether, this wisdom principle has been lost in modern Christianity behind the patriarchal structures, especially the male–focused view of the Incarnation.

> **Key quote**
>
> She is a breath of the power of God, and a pure emanation of the glory of the Almighty.
>
> *The Wisdom of Solomon*, 7:25

Jesus as the incarnation of wisdom

> **Key quote**
>
> The Logos who reveals the 'Father', therefore, was presumed to be properly represented even though the Jewish Wisdom tradition had used the female metaphor, Sophia, for this same idea.
>
> Rosemary Radford Ruether, *Sexism and God-Talk: Toward a Feminist Theology*

Instead, Ruether feels we should recognise in Jesus that feminine aspect of God. Sophia can be found in John's portrayal of Jesus as the Word in *John* 1, in Paul's reference to Jesus as the 'wisdom of God' in 1 *Corinthians* 1 and through a deeper understanding of the role of the Holy Spirit. Ruether believes that this greater understanding will move Christianity in the right direction to understanding that Jesus' maleness was not essential – he could have come as either gender.

Can a male saviour save women?

Yes	No
Jesus can because Jesus was only male by chance – modern Christianity has lost sight of Jesus' feminine/wisdom aspect.	If Jesus is the perfect human then the perfect human is male – there is nothing for women in that statement except the belief that they are less important.
Jesus can because Jesus challenged the warrior-king expectation of his day, which was at the time a traditionally masculine aspect.	Salvation requires us to 'buy in' to the Christian message – why should women be expected to buy in to patriarchy?
At Pentecost, both men and women were equally empowered by the gift of the Saviour, Jesus.	The Christianity that we have inherited is one that drew on male domination, from the Roman Empire onwards.
Jesus engaged with women as much as he did with men – women should have no need to fear that his message and salvation was any less for women than it was for men.	Ruether believed that the Catholic Church's view that women cannot be priests is inherited from Aquinas' view that women are defective – if women are defective in some way, how can they be saved by a male saviour?

Now test yourself

TESTED ☐

7 Which female aspect of God (translated as wisdom) does Ruether think has been lost from Christianity?

8.7 Reinterpretation of God by feminist theologians: Mary Daly

REVISED ☐

'If God is male then the male is God'

As a radical feminist, Daly (1928–2010) felt that it was important to leave established practices behind and aim for a post-Christian spirituality which rejects the male-focused control Christianity has historically had – part of this is the creation of God as a male figure and allowing men to do this has left us with a Christian hierarchy where men have become the top of the chain – 'the male is God'. You cannot simply replace male adjectives about God with female ones – everything requires a complete re-evaluation: God should be castrated.

Christianity's 'Unholy Trinity'

Daly's belief was that the Christian hierarchy was the main reason why women were abused. She believed that this came down to three male power games that were infused into our culture:

1 **Rape**. Not only literally meant (male dominance has led to the thinking that it is permissible to rape or otherwise attack women) but also metaphorically: 'armchair rapists' are those who subscribe to the same approach, perhaps through pornography; ultimately, it is a mentality that the patriarchal society has oppressed women with – often violently.

2 **Genocide**. If rape objectifies a woman then a culture of rape is one in which women are imagined as a group of objects – it sets men as a whole against women as a whole. Genocide is the killing of a large group of people and so the current hierarchical structures place men over women in the same way that genocide sets one group over another.

3 **War**. Daly argued that we live in a world of violence that is based on a 'phallic mentality' – a male-dominated approach that women need to move away from. War is defended as necessary but abortion and euthanasia are rejected – violence for 'good' ends – and so there is hypocrisy in the setup.

Daly said that true rejection of these patriarchal systems requires a total rejection of every existing aspect of culture, because everything comes from a male-dominated sense; everything needs to be rewritten.

Key quote

'God's plan' is often a front for men's plans and a cover for inadequacy, ignorance, and evil.

Mary Daly, *Beyond God the Father*

Spirituality experienced through nature

Daly argued that God, as God is generally thought of, is a fixed, male figure but verbs are better ways of conveying the ongoing and unlimited nature of spirituality. Daly refers to 'be-ing' as life being viewed as a spiritual process instead of aiming to become like a God. Once we move away from objects, we come to a communion with nature. The key to women's spirituality comes from collaboration towards reinventing society.

For Daly, theology and spirituality will not be appropriate for women if one simply changes God the man into God the woman. God is not an object. Because of the issues men face through the corruption of power, they cannot attain spirituality – only those women who have broken away from this can be spiritual beings. Many would reject this, pointing to the vast range of female mystics and saints who have flourished without Daly's approach and would criticise Daly on the grounds of her overemphasis on language – playing games with words to create a desired effect.

8.8 Comparing Ruether and Daly

REVISED ☐

Sexism and patriarchy in Christianity

Both feminist approaches agree that simply to start calling God 'she' and emphasising the feminine aspects of God does not successfully remove the established patriarchy – a patriarchy that Ruether thinks came especially with Christianity and which Daly thought was all-pervading and predated the Old Testament. Both also feel that a side effect of patriarchy has been the assumption that men have power and dominion over nature; both feminist approaches think that only women can save the environment.

Some might suggest that the Christian story is not too male-dominated. Some might say that it is important to read beyond words; others might suggest that the history of Christianity has shaped the Church as it is now and the maleness is part of that process. Indeed, ancient religions all had mother-goddess figures. It could also be observed that Hinduism, which has real devotion to the goddess and female manifestations of the Divine, is no less male-dominated.

Both could also be accused of being selective with the texts they use. There are texts in the Bible that use male language (for example, Father imagery) but female concepts (for example, compassion) and so the Bible as a whole is more balanced than they suggest.

Some key differences include:

- The effect of their common beliefs is very different. Daly advocates a women-centred approach to society, but Ruether does not believe that it is right to sideline men.
- Daly accuses Christianity of being fundamentally sexist and that it therefore needs to be abandoned; Ruether is more positive: change must come from within.

Should Christianity be changed or abandoned?

Some might argue neither. Those who have formed the deepest relationships with God – the mystics, for example – have been both male and female and have done so without reference to gender: God is beyond such things. To what extent is any of this discussion too grounded in human words when dealing with the ineffable divine?

> **Key quote**
>
> We do not have thousands of years to unlearn the wrong patterns that were established over thousands of years.
>
> Rosemary Radford Ruether, *Gaia and God: An Ecofeminist Theology of Earth Healing*

Changed – Ruether	Abandoned – Daly
Men can be brought alongside women to help make the change happen.	Women need to be in control of the change.
The idea that God is both female/male is celebrated.	God can never be understood with gender-language.
God can be maintained and redefined as has happened throughout history – for example, in the way Sophia has been reinterpreted.	God as he is understood currently is to be rejected and replaced by spirituality through the verb that is nature.
The Catholic Church can be changed from within. The people are essentially good and there is sufficient evidence from within the Bible that 'true' teachings can be found.	The Church needs to be rejected. It plays a major part in the Unholy Trinity and is built on sexism and patriarchy.
God the creator ultimately differs from the God that the Church has emphasised.	The Church has gone too far to be saved.

Exam tip

Make sure that you use all the subheadings from the specification (see the beginning of the chapter) to apply the information on this topic in every place that it is relevant – lots of it is transferable!

Now test yourself

TESTED ☐

9 Where does Ruether think that change in the Church should come from?
10 Where does Daly think the way forward for Christianity lies?

8.9 Assessing gender and theology

REVISED ☐

Is Christianity essentially sexist?

Christianity resisted the influences of the Greek and Roman worlds who had both male and female figures as gods and chose its Jewish heritage of one, male God. Jesus deliberately chose men as his key disciples. Some would say:

● Jesus broke every other cultural norm; if he chose only men then there must have been a reason behind it – so it was not a sexist decision but a theological one (women were still part of his inner circle).
● What seems to us as sexist now was not then. It was seen as a real privilege to be in charge of the household and education of the next generation. It is only later cultural (and religious) influences that made Christianity sexist.
● Early Church meetings described in the New Testament clearly have women in leadership roles (for example, Lydia and Sapphira).
● If the Bible is evidence for Christianity being sexist, then perhaps the Bible needs to be understood in its cultural context and we can move away from sexist ideals. Underneath it all the message of Jesus is about breaking away from oppression.

Revision activity

Use the information on each of Ruether and Daly to answer each of the questions in this section from their points of view, using evidence.

Can only women develop a genuine spirituality?

Daly suggested that the maleness of Christianity and the Christian God makes **spirituality** unattainable for women unless they move beyond Christianity. Ruether would disagree and say that there is enough of the feminine in the concept of the divine; it just needs to be rediscovered.

There are countless women who have successfully – and alongside men – developed and written about a spirituality and there are women of note throughout the Bible. However, Daly would accuse this approach of simply trying to carry out a transsexual operation on God – it needs a much deeper change and a very different spirituality.

Can the Christian God be presented in female terms?

The first question is whether God can be presented in terms of gender at all. The Catholic Church says that God is beyond gender and reflects both what we call 'male' and what we call 'female' characteristics at a perfect level.

However, we take for granted the language that calls God a 'he' or 'Father' (because of how our language works and because calling God an 'it' would make God seem less personal) and feminism challenges whether we should do this. Some would say that they can transcend words that are used; others make a conscious decision not to use male pronouns for God; others think that we are too far along the path to be able to have a spiritual relationship with this God.

If the Bible can be reinterpreted or read in a new light, then it is perhaps possible to move away from patriarchal interpretations and it is unlikely that most Christians would have a problem with feminine language being used more about God. This would enable us to rediscover the feminine aspects of the Bible, such as Sophia.

> **Key word**
>
> **Spirituality** Being concerned with the deepest questions of life; being open to the divine

> **Key quote**
>
> In no way is God in man's image. He is neither man nor woman. God is pure spirit in which there is no place for the difference between the sexes.
>
> *Catechism of the Catholic Church*, 370

8.10 Summary and exam tips

REVISED

Exam checklist

- Explain Christian teaching on men and women in the family.
- Explain Christian responses to changing views about men and women in the family and society.
- Analyse *Ephesians* 5:22–33 and *Mulieris Dignitatem* 18–19.
- Analyse Christian views on motherhood/parenthood.
- Analyse Christian views on different types of family.
- Evaluate the idea that Christianity should adapt to society's views of gender.
- Evaluate whether motherhood is liberating or restricting.
- Compare the views about God by Rosemary Radford Ruether and Mary Daly.
- Analyse whether or not Christianity is sexist.
- Evaluate whether only women can develop a genuine spirituality.
- Assess whether or not the Christian God can be presented in female terms.

Sample work

The levels of response for AO2 include one of the hardest skills to learn – the difference between asserting arguments and developing them. Once this is achieved, half the AO2 marks (30 per cent of the total mark for the full A-level) become available to you.

First attempt	Improvement
It might seem that *Ephesians* 5:22–33 is outdated because the culture it describes seems to be typical of the first century.	The first-century text *Ephesians* 5:22–33 certainly seems to reflect the usual household setup of its day. The men are breadwinners and 'in charge' and the women look after the home. However, this puts a modern understanding onto the text: it has been argued that women looking after the home was viewed as equally important to men going out to work or going to the synagogue.

Going further: Women in the Bible

Some of these female characters in the Bible might help you illustrate your writing on this topic. It is also useful to consider whether or not they reflect a patriarchal society.

Eve	First woman, known for being weak to temptation. Punishment for eating the fruit was subservience to man
Hagar	Slave girl of Sarah, Abraham's wife, who bore his first child and then became estranged from the family
Miriam	Prophetess and sister of Moses
Deborah	Powerful prophetess and judge in early Israel
Delilah	Tempted by the Philistines and betrayed the Israelite Samson
Ruth	An example of virtue and loyalty
Esther	An example of prayerfulness and courage who saved the Jewish people from death
Martha	Sister of one of the women called Mary in the Gospels – was criticised by Jesus for busying herself doing domestic chores
Women at the resurrection	In all versions of the resurrection story, it is women who hear first of the empty tomb – they become the first messengers of the resurrection
Phoebe	Early, dedicated helper (or deaconess) in the Church
Lydia	Early convert to Christianity who showed hospitality to Paul and his party
Priscilla	Co-missionary with St Paul, possibly leader of a house church in early Christianity

9 The challenge of secularism

9.1 Introduction

The idea of **secularism** is broadly the idea that religious belief should not affect how the State is run. **Secular** states, such as France and the United States, do exist in what are otherwise very religious countries. Within secularism, there are different approaches; those who simply believe that religion and State decisions should be separated (perhaps to avoid favouring one religion over another) and those who believe that the religious background should be entirely removed from anything to do with the State – from schools to public holidays. There are many Christians who support secularism in its milder sense because Christianity began as a religion that existed within society, not one that controlled society.

Secularisation is the process of making a society more secular, taking religion out of all aspects of State life. Those who support it would say that religion has caused more harm than good in society and also might point to declining church attendance.

> ### Key words
>
> **Secularism** The idea that religious beliefs and institutions should not affect how the State is run; all belief systems are equal in the eyes of the law
>
> **Secular** Worldly or non-religious
>
> **Secularisation** The process of making a society more secular by removing the influence of religious institutions

The specification says

Topic	Content	Key knowledge
The challenge of secularism	● The rise of secularism and secularisation, and the views that:	
	– God is an illusion and the result of wish fulfilment	● the views of Freud and Dawkins that society would be happier without Christianity as it is infantile, repressive and causes conflict
	– Christianity should play no part in public life	● the views of secular humanists that Christian belief is personal and should play no part in public life, including: – education and schools – government and State
	Learners should have the opportunity to discuss issues related to the challenge of secularism, including: ● whether or not spiritual values are just human values ● whether or not there is evidence that Christianity is a major cause of personal and social problems ● whether secularism and secularisation are opportunities for Christianity to develop new ways of thinking and acting ● whether Christianity is, or should be, a significant contributor to society's culture and values.	

Now test yourself

TESTED

1 What is the difference between secularism and secularisation?

9.2 The view that society would be happier without Christianity

Sigmund Freud in the nineteenth and early twentieth century, as well as Richard Dawkins in modern times, argued that the idea of God is an illusion and the result of wish-fulfilment; Christianity is **infantile**, repressive and causes conflict. Both thinkers would advocate secularisation and the development of society towards the removal of religion and the promotion of reason through scientific methods.

Sigmund Freud

Freud (1856–1939) was an atheist psychoanalyst who believed that religion is the cause of **neuroses** and that at some point in the future, science will be able to answer all key questions because psychoanalysis will 'cure' people of religious belief.

- Religion is wish-fulfilment because it is a reflection of our subconscious projecting into our conscious minds – just like a daydream.
- It is an infantile result of the Oedipus Complex (the last stage of a young child's psychological development) because at this stage a boy learns he cannot sexually possess his mother and feels jealousy towards his father; this resentment is repressed into the subconscious mind and projected onto the idea of God, the ultimate father-figure (Freud's analysis of girls was underdeveloped).
- This was expressed in primitive cultures through the totem pole – the phallic symbol of maleness in societies where one went to seek forgiveness; in modern society, this is the male God that we seek comfort from through religious ritual.
- The repetition of this worship is obsessional and found in all parts of society: Freud's famous phrase is that religion is a 'universal obsessional neurosis'.
- Religion is unhealthy and this leads to negativity within society – religion has been the cause of many of society's conflicts.

Richard Dawkins

Dawkins (1941–) is an evolutionary biologist known for his rejection of a need for a creator God, given the evidence for evolution and the increased understanding of scientific principles. This argument has also been offered when discussing the existence of the soul – scientific progress has removed the need to speak of a divine spark or soul in people and unanswered questions should not be filled with an unsubstantiated belief in God, but should be filled with trust that science is on the way to finding answers.

However, Dawkins also thinks that religious belief is problematic for society.

- It causes war and conflict.
- It holds back children – it is a form of child abuse because parents label their children before they can think for themselves.

Problematic are those Christians who believe that evolution and the Big Bang did not happen and that the world was created literally as in the account of the book of *Genesis*: 6000 years ago, in six days and with species in their current form. There is so much evidence against this that for Dawkins it demonstrates their ignorance.

Key words

Infantile Childish; for Freud, this referred to the earliest stage of a person's development

Neurosis A mental illness with symptoms of stress, such as anxiety and obsessive behaviour

Key quote

There is something infantile in the presumption that somebody else (parents in the case of children, God in the case of adults) has a responsibility to give your life meaning and point.

Richard Dawkins, *The God Delusion*

Revision activity

Try making a mind map of the views of both thinkers and look for connections between the two. Enhance your diagram with your class notes, too.

Now test yourself

2 What word for a mental illness did Freud think religion was?
3 What has faith in God been replaced by, according to Dawkins?

9.3 The view that Christian belief should play no part in public life

Secular humanism is a term used for those who think that humans can live positive, good lives without religion. While not necessarily an organised group, humanists have come together to declare common values; those who are humanist hold the full range of views about secularism and secularisation. Ultimately, however, most believe that Christian belief is personal and should play no part in public life.

Education and schools

Approximately one-third of schools in the United Kingdom are faith schools, mainly with Church of England or Roman Catholic foundations. Dawkins is a clear opponent of faith education and believes that it is time for them to be replaced.

Arguments for faith schools	Arguments against faith schools
Only one-third of schools are faith schools, so families still have choice.	It is labelling children from a young age.
Church attendance might be dropping but many more people still consider themselves Christian and should be allowed to reflect this in their educational choices.	The teaching of some areas, such as RE and science, might be subject to bias, especially in fundamentalist schools, possibly even leading to a risk of radicalisation.
All schools have mission statements and value systems of one sort or another so faith schools are no different from other schools.	Children in faith schools are not fully aware of the rest of secular society.
It reflects diversity and tolerance – fundamental British values.	Faith schools might reflect some people's narrow views of what religious people are like.
Pupils in faith schools are as diverse as the societies they exist in; they are not necessarily made up only of their faith background.	Faith should be something only taught by parents and religious communities.

Government and State

The United Kingdom historically has close ties between Christianity and the State. The Church of England is a national Church and the Queen is its Supreme Governor. Some bishops have automatic seats in the House of Lords. Some argue that these historic links should be separated because it would reflect the reality of twenty-first century Britain. Others believe that this is still representative of how the country is made up, and representatives from faith traditions outside the Church of England are now represented in the House of Lords as well.

The United States and France entirely separate Church and State.

It has been argued that secularisation of State can lead to the censorship of certain approaches in favour of a different, non-religious ideology, which is still itself an ideology: it could be argued that this led to fascism and communism. A more balanced approach to secularism can celebrate all perspectives, including religious ones.

Some Christians would argue that the religion that Jesus founded was one where Christians spoke from within their secular context and worked together to promote the common good and to care for those in need.

> **Key quote**
>
> Let everyone be subject to the governing authorities, for there is no authority except that which God has established. The authorities that exist have been established by God.
>
> *Romans* 13:1

Now test yourself

4 Approximately what proportion of British schools are faith schools?

5 Name two countries that completely separate Church and State.

9.4 Is Christianity a major cause of personal and social problems?

Some accusations

- Christianity has been the cause of warfare when it has tried to gain supremacy over other traditions, such as in the Crusades.
- Christianity rejects the indisputable advances of science and holds society back – for example, in its beliefs about the soul.
- Some ethical stances of Christians do not match with modern society, such as views about homosexuality.
- Any absolutist approach to life is intolerant of the views of others and damaging to society; for example, in Christian views on euthanasia, which do not allow people the freedom to make their own choices about their lives.
- Christians can radicalise converts as much as any other religion.
- Christianity is patriarchal and oppresses women.
- Christianity promotes beliefs in things that hold people back from reality and stop personal development – for example, in beliefs about life after death.
- Christianity (along with other institutions) has suffered from the child abuse scandal and has not reacted appropriately to accusations, suggesting that it thinks it is untouchable in some way.
- Christians place their trust in a Bible that is outdated and which seems to condone practices like slavery.
- Differing beliefs can divide families, perhaps when one member converts to Christianity.
- Some Christian evangelists do so to earn money, not to preach a faith.

> **Revision activity**
>
> As you go through this list, examine it critically and decide whether it is fair to judge the whole of Christianity by each accusation. What responses might a Christian give to each one? For example, the Crusades might be dismissed as long ago in history and the Church's structures now are very different than they were then.

Some responses

Christians would emphasise that they are a community that is always seeking the ideal way to live, perhaps based on Jesus' commandment to love, but that it is a community that is made up of humans who fall short of God's ways of perfection. It is wrong to judge the redeeming work of Jesus Christ against human beings.

Some Christians would reject denominations other than their own and say that the divided Church might be the cause of problems, but their own denomination would not cause these issues. They might suggest that a society where their denomination has more control would be more harmonious.

It is possible to challenge some of the concerns about Christian ethics by asking the question of whether something becomes right if society begins to accept it. If the majority of society began to accept the torture of children, would that make it right? Some Christians hold fast to their beliefs about homosexuality, abortion, capital punishment and other contentious issues because they believe that they are wrong for all time.

Christians would point to all the good that the Church has offered the world: educating the poor, working abroad, supporting the civil rights movement (for example, Martin Luther King), food banks – as well as the work churches do on a local level. Christians are called to work for the good of society and also to be distinctive within society – to challenge where injustice is seen.

> **Key quote**
>
> Let anyone who is without sin be the first to throw a stone at her.
>
> *John 8:7*

Now test yourself

6 Why might some Christians resist the changing ethical standards of the twenty-first century?

9.5 Are secularism and secularisation opportunities for Christianity?

Over the course of Christianity's history, it has had to adapt to different ways of thinking and it might be argued that, with the speed of change over the last generation, it is important that Christianity is open to changing again. The pace of change in scientific understanding, the results of the brutalities of twentieth-century violence and twenty-first century extremism have all moved people away from organised religion.

However, some Christians would argue that now, more than ever, it is time for Christians to stand up for the truth revealed through Christ and the Bible and to resist this move towards change. They might argue that if Christianity is sidelined, it might lead to the religion being able to affect the lives of far fewer people.

Some might use the opportunity to analyse why society is attracted to this change and to try to look for opportunities for evangelism or education about Christianity. Others, reflecting fear by many in society over the pace of change, might focus on the traditional aspects of Christianity, especially its focus on spiritual things over material ones.

The earliest Christian community saw itself as living within the secular State, not opposed to it; modern Christians might be inspired by this when thinking about their place in society.

Revision activity

Present the information in Section 9.5 in a diagram format that you find useful. Add your own views.

Making links

For ideas about inter-faith dialogue, which might overlap in this section, see Chapter 7.

If society moves towards full secularisation, some Christians would choose to embrace this as an opportunity to speak without fear of being sidelined as a minority view or one view among many. It could start to be distinctive, separate from the State. However, others would say that this would make Christians more likely to be left on one side and the conflicting ideologies that place science, materialism and perhaps capitalism at the centre of life would undermine the purpose of life, which is found and fully understood within Christianity.

In terms of the UK Government in particular, some might suggest that removing the Christian influence would be more tolerant towards non-Christian members. It might be argued that the Christian elements of the Houses of Parliament (such as starting each sitting with Christian prayers) are ritualistic only and are not necessary to the smooth running of government. Some might argue that an elected House of Lords would be more democratic than the current system, thus removing religious representation from the upper chamber. However, others might suggest that the UK as an entity exists because of its history and traditions and so it would be wrong to lose this. Christians might say that having representation in the House of Lords helps to safeguard against immoral legislation.

Now test yourself

7 Why might a Christian feel that Christianity shouldn't be sidelined in matters of State?

9.6 Assessing secularism

Are spiritual values just human values?

The fullest list of humanist values can be found in the 2002 Amsterdam Declaration. Their list of seven core values include many things that most, if not all, religious believers would identify as spiritual values: ethics, rationality, human rights, social responsibility, fulfilment and the importance of creativity. At this level, spiritual values and human values are very similar. Equally, the Ten Commandments have many core ethical demands that are universal – you do not need to be religious to follow those that are not about God.

Some Christian values, however, do differ from these. Upholding the dignity of life over personal choice (for example, when considering euthanasia) and loving your enemies are examples of values that make Christianity distinctive, but would not be shared by all humanists.

Christians might argue that human values tend to be shared on a worldly level, but that there is an additional layer or dimension to Christian, spiritual values; one that sees an ultimate purpose or reason, a world beyond this one and a creator God who loves and sustains the world and wants people to worship him.

It could also be argued that there are no such things as human values. It is very difficult to achieve a complete sense of what a list of human values might look like, especially when considering the vast range of people around the globe.

> **Making links**
>
> Consider how Christian ethics compares with the ethical theories you studied and which are covered in the Religion and Ethics book, Chapters 1–4. Where do they agree and disagree?

Should Christianity be a significant contributor to society's culture and values?

Richard Dawkins does not think that Christianity's contribution to British society should be ignored. He praised the literary legacy of the King James Bible, for example. However, he does not think that Christianity should be a driving force in shaping the society of tomorrow because it is time we moved beyond religious ideals.

Christianity should be a contributor	Counter-argument
Britain today would not be the country it is without Christianity.	Britain today and tomorrow is much more multi-cultural than fifty years ago.
Our artistic heritage, such as art, architecture, literature and music, owes so much to Christianity.	There is wonderful heritage in non-Christian artistic cultures.
Christianity can contribute without being dominant in the conversation.	All religious voices need to be moved away from in order to move forward in society.
Christian ethics on a human level are ethics that apply to all, not just Christians.	If this is the case then the ethics do not need to be distinctively Christian.

It might seem impossible that Christianity can expect to contribute to society as an institution because society is made up of individuals who have different approaches and Christianity is only one of these approaches, so should not expect to be treated specially; a harmonious society seems to require all individuals to be celebrated.

Some Christians, however, might suggest that they have a 'right' to drive the agenda forward both in government and legislation, as well as in cultural circles because they represent true belief, or because Christianity is the majority faith in the UK. Ultimately, it will be what approach individual Churches and Christians take that helps others judge how appropriate it is.

Now test yourself

TESTED

8 What is the name of the 2002 Declaration that lists seven core humanist principles?
9 What seventeenth-century Christian text does Richard Dawkins praise for its literary value to society?

9.7 Summary and exam tips

REVISED

Exam checklist

- Explain secularism and secularisation.
- Explain the thinking of Freud on religion.
- Explain the views of Dawkins on religion.
- Assess whether Christianity should play a part in public life.
- Evaluate whether there is a difference between human and spiritual values.
- Critically assess whether Christianity is a cause of personal and social problems.
- Evaluate the role of Christianity in tomorrow's society.

Sample work

When dealing with complex material, it is important to ensure that you write accurately, precisely and with some deep engagement in the ideas. It is useful to try to force yourself not to write short sentences or groups of ideas and to ensure that you expand a point fully before moving on to the next point. Here, two brief points are replaced by one significant exploration of a point.

First attempt	Improvement
Christianity has created many problems within society. It has led to wars and oppression of people, such as women.	Christianity could be argued to have created a number of problems within society over the years. For example, its patriarchal approach to authority has led to women being devalued in much of the Church's history. It might be said that Christians have begun to move beyond this, but this is certainly not universal.

Going further: Quotations to consider

The reality is in fact such that certain forms of behaviour and thinking are being presented as the only reasonable ones and, therefore, as the only appropriately human ones. Christianity finds itself exposed now to an intolerant pressure that at first ridicules it – as belonging to a perverse, false way of thinking – and then tries to deprive it of breathing space in the name of an ostensible rationality.

Pope Benedict XVI

Exam tip

Don't feel you must write out lengthy quotations. If you like one or more of these examples, be ready to summarise it as part of an argument.

We want a world where everyone lives cooperatively on the basis of shared human values, respect for human rights, and concern for future generations. We want non-religious people to be confident in living ethical and fulfilling lives on the basis of reason and humanity.

British Humanist Association

So it is possible to imagine a 'procedurally' secular society and legal system which is always open to being persuaded by confessional or ideological argument on particular issues, but is not committed to privileging permanently any one confessional group. The recent UK debate about legalising assisted dying brought into focus many of these matters in a quite sharp way.

Rowan Williams, former Archbishop of Canterbury

If I were a dictator, religion and state would be separate. I swear by my religion. I will die for it. But it is my personal affair. The state has nothing to do with it. The state would look after your secular welfare, health, communications, foreign relations, currency and so on, but not your or my religion. That is everybody's personal concern!

Mahatma Gandhi, Indian Independence leader

Some people believe the alternative to bad religion is secularism, but that's wrong ... The answer to bad religion is better religion – prophetic rather than partisan, broad and deep instead of narrow, and based on values as opposed to ideology.

Jim Wallace, American Christian writer

10 Liberation theology and Marx

10.1 Introduction

A Christian base community is a community that brings together the poor and oppressed and feeds them, provides pastoral care, teaches them the basics of faith and so on. As such, these communities feel in control of their faith and beliefs and people are empowered to feel active parts of the Church, from the base/bottom upwards, even if the nearest church and priest are miles away. In Latin America, these base communities play a real part in establishing the solidarity required for making a significant change in the lives of the poor. Liberation theology likewise works from the base upwards, focusing on the real needs of the community and emphasising good action before deep theology. Much of this approach comes from the influence of Marxism, but liberation theologians are divided about how influential Marxism should be within Christianity.

> **Key quote**
>
> We believe that from the transcendence of the Gospel, we can assess what the life of the poor consists of and we also believe that placing ourselves on the side of the poor and attempting to give them life we will know what the eternal truth of the Gospel consists of.
>
> Oscar Romero, speech, February 1980

The specification says

Topic	Content	Key knowledge
Liberation theology and Marx	• The relationship of liberation theology and Marx, including: – Marx's teaching on alienation and exploitation	• Alienation occurs when humans are dehumanised and unable to live fulfilling lives • Exploitation occurs when humans are treated as objects and used as a means to an end
	– liberation theology's use of Marx to analyse social sin	• Liberation theology's use of Marxist analysis to analyse the deeper or 'structural' causes of social sin that have resulted in poverty, violence and injustice, including: – capitalism – institutions (for example, schools, churches, the State)
	– liberation theology's teaching on the 'preferential option for the poor'	• The view that Gospel demands that Christians must give priority to the poor and act in solidarity with them, including implications of this: – placing right action (orthopraxis) before official Church teaching (orthodoxy)
	Learners should have the opportunity to discuss issues related to liberation theology and Marx, including: • whether or not Christian theology should engage with atheist secular ideologies • whether or not Christianity tackles social issues more effectively than Marxism • whether or not liberation theology has engaged with Marxism fully enough • whether or not it is right for Christians to prioritise one group over another.	

Now test yourself

TESTED

1 In the liberation theology approach, what comes before theology?

10.2 Marx's teachings

The teachings of Karl Marx (1818–1883) are best understood through his underpinning principle of **praxis**:

- Society is constantly changing through history: going through conflict, stability and then conflict again.
- Change comes about through analysing a situation.
- Then working out the reasons behind it.
- Then changing it.

Alienation and exploitation

After an initial period of harmony, society broke down and people are now in competition with one another; they are means to ends – objectified. So, humans became dehumanised and were unable to live fulfilling lives – exploitation. Marx identified some key factors in this concept:

- Religion and belief in God has brainwashed people into thinking that God is the cause behind change in the world, rather than physical processes – this is an illusion that causes false hopes in people (for example, an afterlife).
- Religion tells people that some people are born to rule over other people and that everything will be equalised in the afterlife. This objectifies some people and **alienates** them.
- Capitalism, which is driven by profit, makes some people objectify others (such as workers being 'owned' by the ruling classes); society would be better off under communism, where everyone shares equally.
- The production line makes everyone depersonalised and therefore alienated; workers simply 'make', not create, are paid and then have to spend their earnings in places owned by the ruling classes.

The fewer ruling classes (bourgeoisie) control the many workers (proletariat) who are alienated, exploited and objectified. Religion is an additional tool to ensure that they are kept in their place, with the promise of a better future in the afterlife. In Marx's analysis of history, he saw times when the workers had tried to resist this way of life, but had been met by violence and, in his view, the society of his time demonstrated this very specifically.

Marx said that religion is one of the more powerful tools to oppress the workers: 'Religion is the sigh of the oppressed creature, the heart of a heartless world, and the soul of soulless conditions. It is the opiate of the people' (from the introduction to a book on Hegel). Opium as a drug was used to dull pain and get away from the troubles of this world. The alienated and exploited people were 'given' religion in the same way.

Praxis is therefore required. Marx believed that, having reflected on the causes of alienation, an uprising would need to take place to install communism as the right way for society to exist and to reject the capitalist machine.

> **Key words**
>
> **Praxis** Understanding a situation and then bringing about change in it; a critical reflective process that moves from theory to action
>
> **Alienation** The estrangement of people from what they are meant to be; degrading a person into a thing or object or making a person give up their proper place in society

> **Exam tip**
>
> Make sure you carefully link the information about Marx to the argument required by the question set – don't just write out his theory.

> **Making links**
>
> How does what Marx says affect your study of business ethics? See the Religion and Ethics book, Chapter 6.

Now test yourself

2 For Marx, what word means to degrade someone into an object?
3 What is the difference between capitalism and communism?

10.3 Liberation theology

Analysis of social sin

The uprising that Marx said was required seemed, in the 1970s, to be taking place in Latin America, where many poor people were under the control of oppressive governments; workers were alienated; capitalism and industrialisation were prioritised. Industrialisation filtered into key institutions, including schools and the State, as well as the Church.

Gustavo Gutierrez (1928–) is a central figure in the foundation of liberation theology. He believes his theology has been influenced by Marxism, though most liberation theologians are quick to point out that there is only one true teacher, Jesus, and that Marxism is an 'instrument' that helps the methodology of liberation theology.

Liberation theology believes that the Christian must not stand back; the class struggle is too great. Society has inequality at its heart – structural inequality – and this leads to structural sin – the social sin that is deeper than any individual sin. Capitalism has not worked and liberation theology believes that praxis is required to change these structures. Socialism is the best of the current alternatives, though still not ideal.

- Structural sin is the ultimate form of alienation because every member of society is alienated.
- It is also something Christians are familiar with because of the idea of Original Sin – humans are corrupted and need to break away from it as much as possible.

Liberation theology embraces the idea, found in Luke's Gospel in particular, of **reversal**. One of Luke's themes is social justice and the social revolution that Christianity promised. The Kingdom of God is not in the distant heaven, but among us. To read Christianity the way many commentators think Luke wanted means:

- Theology starts with the earth and people, not with doctrine or God.
- The poor (proletariat) become drivers for action (praxis).

The **hermeneutic of suspicion** is considered useful in liberation theology. As a way of interpreting the Bible, it places a Marxist reading on texts and applies them to the needs of an alienated society.

In 1979, a meeting of Latin American bishops made the following points about structural sin:

- The Church needs to challenge social sin as much as individual sins.
- The Church must not mirror the oppressive bourgeoisie and should let the people have a say in its decisions.
- The Church needs to re-find itself as a community, not as an institution.

Preferential option for the poor

Preferential option for the poor reflects the core message of the parable of the Sheep and the Goats, that humans will be judged based on their recognition of Jesus in the needy. The phrase implies that the Gospel demands that Christians must give priority to the poor (when they can: it is aimed at the rich and influential) and act in solidarity with them (in the same way that Jesus did). It can be justified in five ways:

- God is a living God who seeks justice for his people.
- Jesus worked for the poor.
- We will be judged based on our response to the poor.

Revision activity

Try rewriting these notes to categorise the points into areas where you feel liberation theology is strong and where it is weak. Try to justify why you have done this.

Key quote

The denunciation of injustice implies the rejection of the use of Christianity to legitimise the established order.

Gustavo Gutierrez, *A Theology of Liberation*

Key words

Reversal The idea that justice in the Kingdom of God is about reversing the opportunities of those on earth (for example, the poor shall become rich)

Hermeneutic of suspicion The process of interpreting the Bible (hermeneutics) by asking questions that have not been asked before to challenge traditional or official interpretations; in the context of liberation theology, its focus is on economic motivations

Making links

For more on the parable of the Sheep and the Goats, see Chapter 2.

Key word

Preferential option for the poor The idea that the needs of the poor must be prioritised at all times

- The first Apostles looked after the poor.
- Christians should work for the common good and try to transform society.

Christians should not stand by when presented with injustice or human suffering as all people are made in God's image and likeness. Inspired by Marx, liberation theologians prioritise action, called **orthopraxis**, over belief (**orthodoxy**).

Liberation theology places orthopraxis before orthodoxy. In terms of the preferential option for the poor, this places feeding the hungry before making them believe in key aspects of the faith or before being obedient to the rules of the Church. Therefore, the preferential option for the poor starts with the reality 'on the ground' and works from there.

Orthopraxis starts with living among the poor, in solidarity, visiting and caring for them as much as teaching them. After this, it is possible to explore the context of the people 'on the ground': why are they poor? How does the Bible speak into this context? What action must be taken?

The Kingdom of God must be brought about on earth for those who are alienated and live in poverty. For some, this has been interpreted as requiring violent struggle: Camilo Torres Restrepo, a Catholic priest, joined the Columbian National Liberation Army and was killed in action, standing up for the oppressed.

Key quote

If Jesus were alive today, he would be a guerrillero.
Camilo Torres Restrepo

Gutierrez did not promote violence, but did not reject it outright. He said that liberation takes place over two stages, both of which are essential.
1 Fixing the human-made problems of poverty and oppression through human methods – liberating them from structural sin.
2 Liberating people from personal sin and promoting reconciliation.

Some liberation theologians suggest that spiritual liberation should come first, such as Juan Segundo, who argued that Christians can definitely free people from personal sin, but may or may not be able to change social structures.

Exam tip

Make sure you can represent the full range of approaches to liberation theology in your essays.

The Catholic Church has taken time officially to welcome liberation theology. Pope John Paul II endorsed the phrase 'preferential option for the poor' but also emphasised spiritual poverty alongside material poverty. Pope Benedict XVI was suspicious of the Marxist influences and (before he became Pope) argued that the Catholic Church would work for the poor but not using Marxism as a tool. Pope Francis, who comes from Latin America, has endorsed much of liberation theology, although distanced himself from the Marxist aspects of it. He himself lives a simple lifestyle and has criticised capitalism. In 2015, he named Oscar Romero, the Archbishop of San Salvador who was killed as a liberation theologian, a martyr of the Church.

Now test yourself

TESTED

4 What phrase is used by liberation theologians to describe the failings that are ingrained into institutions?
5 In which Gospel is the theme of reversal found most prominently?
6 What does the phrase 'preferential option for the poor' mean?

10.4 Assessing liberation theology

Should Christian theology engage with atheist secular ideologies?

Some Christians would argue that Christian theology should keep away from atheist ideologies. In the example of liberation theology and Marxism, there is some suspicion about a worldview that begins with a rejection of God and religion as one of the key tools of oppression. Here there is a direct contradiction between a fundamental aspect of Church teaching and a key element of Marxism. The Church should be prepared to remain distinctive and not try to assimilate with such beliefs because it would suggest that truth can be found outside the revelation of Jesus Christ and the Bible.

However, those Christians who take a natural theology approach might say that reason can be (partially) accurate outside the Church. In this case, it is right for Christianity to engage with other ideologies, even if only to use them as tools to help its own reflection.

The key to this question is what it means to 'engage' with an ideology. Many Christians would say that they should not be afraid of discussion and debate. However, others would say that the Bible contains all that is required to live life and no outside discussion is necessary.

> **Exam tip**
>
> It is important to note that the question here is about Christian theology in general, rather than liberation theology specifically.

Does Christianity tackle social issues more effectively than Marxism?

Some might accuse Christianity of being too gentle when it comes to tackling poverty and oppression, and would argue that the revolutionary uprising approach of Marxism is the only way to bring about significant change. However, where revolutions have brought about communism, it is debatable whether this approach has been entirely successful.

Christianity accepts that suffering is a part of life and tries to engage with that at every level, but it is most effective when it does so at a local level. Where Christianity is most effective is where each individual responds to the need to build the Kingdom of God in their own context, rather than the Marxist approach of tackling society on a larger scale.

The key difference between Christianity and Marxism is, of course, the spiritual dimension. Christians would argue that the reality of God can touch people's lives in a very real way; Marx rejects religion and says it is too focused on the afterlife. Christians might say that religion is more about people in this world than about the afterlife.

> **Typical mistake**
>
> Avoid making sweeping generalisations when discussing social issues. Be specific, with examples, and remember that other parts of the world are very different to the UK!

> **Key quote**
>
> When I give food to the poor, they call me a saint. When I ask why the poor have no food, they call me a communist.
>
> Archbishop Helder Camara, in Z. Rocha, *Helder, the Gift*

Has liberation theology engaged enough with Marxism?

Most liberation theologians see Marxism as a tool to help reinterpret the Christian message in a specific context. However, as we have seen, there is the full range of approaches to this question.

There has not been enough engagement	There has been too much engagement
Marxism calls for an uprising; Christianity does not seem to have made enough impact doing it more gently.	Communism has been shown to be unsuccessful and so Christianity should not have linked itself with this approach.
There has been too much attention to Marx's atheism – more thought about the causes of alienation and ways to tackle this would create deeper changes.	Liberation theology has lost sight of Jesus' death on the cross, which liberates people from sin first and foremost.
Many of the processes of the two ideologies are similar: the importance of analysing history, the importance of working towards a better future.	Liberation theology argues that praxis will bring about change; the Christian message should be that God's grace will bring this about.
Fear of Marx's atheism or promotion of violence has led his approach to be diluted too much; Christians now talk about spiritual poverty and don't place enough focus on real, material poverty.	Liberation theology has skewed the debate: it suggests that it is the only way to counteract issues in society, whereas society is significantly more complex than this approach suggests.
Christianity needs to understand from Marx the importance of re-evaluating society in each new stage of history – it can then have an impact even beyond the current aims of liberation theology, such as in modern secular society.	Marxism contains areas that deny the importance of the individual and that deny God's existence. It is too dangerous to engage with some of it as it might lead to unorthodox beliefs entering the Church.

Is it right for Christians to prioritise one group over another?

Liberation theology very specifically prioritises the poor and oppressed over other groups. The Bible is clear that God works for the poor and needy and Jesus came to bring salvation to outcasts. However, it is not just the poor who are outcasts. This might be behind Pope John Paul's call to widen the scope to the spiritual poor as much as the materially poor.

As Jesus taught in the parable of the Rich Man and Lazarus (*Luke* 16:19–31), the rich need as much salvation as anyone else. In this parable, the rich man who ignores the poor Lazarus at his gate ends up in hell and he is told that he had the opportunity to prevent this if he'd paid more attention to the teachings of the Scriptures. Arguably, liberation theology could be over-emphasising the poor to the detriment of the rich: Jesus died for all people. A response might be that it is not so much the rich that are condemned for being rich, but those rich people who do not help the oppressed.

The different Gospel writers all present the Jesus story in slightly different ways, probably because they were emphasising different things for the different communities they were writing for. Perhaps Christians need to follow their lead and consider who those most in need are in their own communities – at a local level – and then, at this local level, to prioritise those who need it.

> **Key quote**
>
> Jesus said, 'It is not the healthy who need a doctor, but the sick. I have not come to call the righteous, but sinners.'
>
> *Mark 2:17*

Now test yourself

TESTED

7 Why might some Christians reject outright the idea that there are things to learn from other ideologies outside the Church?
8 What is the main stumbling block between Christianity and Marxism?
9 Which Pope felt that the message of liberation theology could be widened to encompass the poor in spirit?

10.5 Summary and exam tips

Exam checklist

- Explain Marx's teaching on alienation and exploitation.
- Explain how liberation theology uses the thinking of Marx.
- Explain liberation theology's teaching on 'preferential option for the poor'.
- Assess the approach of placing orthopraxis before orthodoxy.
- Evaluate the relationship between Christianity and atheist ideologies.
- Critically compare Christian and Marxist responses to social issues.
- Evaluate whether liberation theology has sufficiently engaged with Marxism.
- Critically assess whether it is right for Christians to prioritise one group over another.

Sample work

The key to scoring highly in this examination is your ability to analyse and evaluate the material you present in relation to the question. Don't get drawn in to thinking you have to write everything you know about a topic, especially when a question is narrow in its scope. Everyone has the same length of time to write an essay and so your essay will be marked with this in mind.

First attempt	Improvement
Liberation theology came out of Latin America where there are many poor people who are oppressed by their governments. Gustavo Gutierrez is an example of a liberation theologian. He believed that Marx influenced his thinking, but that he has not become a Marxist. This could be good because Marxism is an atheistic ideology and this stands in direct contrast to Christianity.	Christianity and Marxism differ in the fact that Marxism rejects God and religion from the outset as a means of controlling the proletariat. This implies that the two cannot work together in any way because Christianity could not be seen to link to an ideology that is atheistic. However, prominent liberation theologian Gustavo Gutierrez would say that his views have been influenced by Marxism, but that he is not himself a Marxist. It is possible for one ideology to influence and change another and therefore potentially Christianity and Marxism could work together.

Going further: Reading the Bible with liberation theology

Applying liberation theology's hermeneutic of suspicion to Biblical texts can be a useful way to engage fully with the approach that liberation theology takes. Here are some examples that could get you started:

- When God says that he has heard of the misery of his people in Egypt (*Exodus* 3:7) and he is concerned about their suffering, he is speaking as much to the poor and oppressed in Latin America as he was to the Israelites in Egypt. God offered a way of breaking free towards a promised better future.
- The rich man and Lazarus story in *Luke* 16:19–31 makes us question how the rich man became rich and analyse how even in Jesus' time the alienation of the proletariat was taken for granted.
- Paul's very short letter to Philemon shows him pleading for good care of the slave Onesimus. What does this letter say about slavery and the Christian response to it?

Now test yourself answers at **www.hoddereducation.co.uk/myrevisionnotes**

Glossary

Agape The unconditional love God has for humans that humans need to try to reflect

Alienation The estrangement of people from what they are meant to be; degrading a person into a thing or object or making a person give up their proper place in society

Anonymous Christian Someone who is open to God's grace but not a Christian

Beatific vision The state of eternal happiness when we are face-to-face with God

Concupiscence The idea that our natural perfected state has been wounded so that we are not bad, but always inclining towards sin

Conscience The inner sense of right and wrong in a person, sometimes described as an internal voice

Costly grace The idea that the free gift of grace demands a response of true, sacrificial discipleship – total abandonment to Christ and to be Christ-like in your attitude

Deontological Duty-based approaches to ethics

Divinity The divine aspect of Jesus – the part of Jesus that is God

Double predestination The view (held by Calvinists) that God chooses those who will go to heaven and also those who will go to hell

Election Being chosen by God for heaven or hell

Evangelism Spreading the Christian message

Fall The moment when Adam and Eve disobeyed God by eating the fruit of the forbidden tree; humans are 'fallen' because of this moment

Final judgement The judgement of all nations at the end of time

Forgive To let go of past anger and move on in life

Grace God's generous, undeserved and free act of love for the world through Jesus (and despite concupiscence)

Hermeneutic of suspicion The process of interpreting the Bible (hermeneutics) by asking questions that have not been asked before to challenge traditional or official interpretations; in the context of liberation theology, its focus is on economic motivations

Human nature The essential sense of what all humans are like; shared characteristics

Human will For Augustine, given to humans by God at creation and used to make choices. It is driven by self-love and generous love, which work together to help people choose to love God properly

Incarnation God becoming a human being in Jesus Christ

Infantile Childish; for Freud, this referred to the earliest stage of a person's development

Innate Natural. An innate human sense of the divine is something we are born with, not one we acquire

Liberator Someone who frees a person or group of people

Limited election The view that only some people are chosen to be saved

Morals A set of principles linked to doing right actions

Natural theology Use of reason and observation of the world to come to a knowledge of God

Neurosis A mental illness with symptoms of stress, such as anxiety and obsessive behaviour

Non-propositional revelation The idea that God does not reveal himself through truth statements, so the revelation might need interpretation

Normative way to salvation The usual or ideal way to be saved, but not necessarily the only one

Original Sin The state that humans were brought into by the Fall, which was the first sin

Orthodoxy Right belief; the official beliefs of the Church

Orthopraxis Right actions

Parousia Used of the second coming of Christ, when Jesus will return to judge the world

Particular judgement Individual judgement at the moment of death

Patriarchy Male-dominated; a patriarchal society is one where men have more power than women

Praxis Understanding a situation and then bringing about change in it; a critical reflective process that moves from theory to action

Predestination The idea that God chooses and guides some people to salvation

Preferential option for the poor The idea that the needs of the poor must be prioritised at all times

Propositional revelation The idea that God reveals himself in truth statements. To say that the Bible is an example of this is to say that the Bible is a series of truth statements

Purgatory The (mainly) Catholic belief in a state of cleansing that takes place before someone enters heaven

Religionless Christianity Bonhoeffer's idea that Christianity should get rid of old-fashioned ideas and separate itself from present ideologies

Repent To turn your life in a new direction, away from your past life

Restricted access exclusivism Salvation comes from hearing the Christian message and accepting it into your life

Revealed theology The idea that God reveals what we need to know about him to us in different ways – for example, through the Bible or the person of Jesus

Revelation Literally uncovering something that was previously hidden

Reversal The idea that justice in the Kingdom of God is about reversing the opportunities of those on earth (for example, the poor shall become rich)

Secular Worldly or non-religious

Secularisation The process of making a society more secular by removing the influence of religious institutions

Secularism The idea that religious beliefs and institutions should not affect how the State is run; all belief systems are equal in the eyes of the law

Sensus divinitas A sense of God, used by Calvin to talk about an innate sense in each of us

Sin Turning away from the will of God

Single predestination The view (held by Catholics) that God chooses those who will go to heaven

Social cohesion A society that works well together – has a sense of identity and community

Solidarity The idea that Christians must be 'for others'

Spirituality Being concerned with the deepest questions of life; being open to the divine

Summum bonum Highest or greatest good

Theology of religion The branch of theology that examines the status of different religions in relation to each other

Universal access exclusivism The idea that God wishes everyone to be saved

Universalism The view that everyone will be saved

Unlimited election The view that everyone is called to be saved but only a few will be